Cop in the Hood

COP IN THE HOOD

My Year Policing Baltimore's
Eastern District

PETER MOSKOS

PRINCETON UNIVERSITY PRESS
PRINCETON AND OXFORD

Copyright © 2008 by Princeton University Press

Requests for permission to reproduce material from this work should be sent to Permissions, Princeton University Press

Published by Princeton University Press, 41 William Street, Princeton, New Jersey 08540

In the United Kingdom: Princeton University Press, 3 Market Place, Woodstock, Oxfordshire OX20 1SY

All Rights Reserved

Library of Congress Cataloging-in-Publication Data

Moskos, Peter, 1971–
    Cop in the hood : my year policing Baltimore's eastern district / Peter Moskos.
        p. cm.
    Includes bibliographical references and index.
    ISBN 978-0-691-12655-5
    1. Moskos, Peter, 1971– 2. Police—Maryland—Baltimore—Biography.
I. Title.
HV7911.M644A3 2008
363.2092—dc22
[B]   2007045211

British Library Cataloging-in-Publication Data is available

This book has been composed in Janson text

Printed on acid-free paper. ∞

press.princeton.edu

Printed in the United States of America

1 3 5 7 9 10 8 6 4 2

Crystal Sheffield and I sat next to each other in the police academy. When the rest of the class would mope and whine, Crystal refused to take part in the petty games common among fifty people cooped up in the same room for too long. "I love everybody here," she would say. She meant it, too. Always smiling (except when pointing out that I ate too much garlic), she was police for all the right reasons. Sheffield died on duty, August 22, 2002. My sympathies go to her entire family, especially her son and sister, both of whom inspired her deeply.

This book is dedicated to her and the nine other Baltimore City Police Officers killed in the line-of-duty since my brief tenure: Officer Jamie Allen Roussey, March 8, 2000; Officer Kevon Malik Gavin, April 21, 2000; Officer Kevin Joseph McCarthy and Sergeant John David Platt, October 14, 2000; Agent Michael J. Cowdery, March 13, 2001; Crystal Deneen Sheffield, August 22, 2002; Detective Thomas G. Newman, November 23, 2002; Officer Brian Donte Winder, July 3, 2004; Officer Anthony A. Byrd, May 19, 2006; Detective Troy Lamont Chesley, Sr., January 9, 2007.

10–7. May they rest in peace.

Contents

Acknowledgments

Without the emotional and financial support of my parents, Ilca and Charles Moskos, I could not have begun nor finished my book.

To the warm and welcoming people of Baltimore, thank you. You make Baltimore the wonderful city I love.

I thank the Baltimore Police Department and Baltimore's former mayor, Maryland governor Martin O'Malley, for letting me conduct this research.

Orlando Patterson and Chris Winship steered me through the minefield of graduate school. Maurice Punch and John Van Maanen, in particular, sparked my interest in police. Their never-wavering enthusiasm kept me going through it all.

I thank my sergeant, the police academy class of "99–5," and my squadmates who backed me up. I wish everybody a speedy and successful retirement.

I thank and remember Miss Mary Ballis for giving me a home in Baltimore, Miss Joyce for keeping Eager Street clean, and Mr. George Watson for hot coffee on cold mornings.

I am indebted to Tim Sullivan for his vision and editing skills.

I deeply appreciate the advice, support, and time given by Elijah Anderson, Howard Becker, Katch Belash, Gwendolyn Dordick, Amy Eckert, Robert Emerson, Maki Haberfeld, John Gavrilis, Gabriella Gonzalez, Peter Holla, James Jacobs, Delores Jones-Brown, Jack Katz, George Kelling, Carl Klockars, Rien Maas, Saskia Maas, Peter Manning,

Peter Marudas, Laura Miller, Andrew Moskos, Zora O'Neill, Jacqueline Pica, Yolande Robins, Jon Rosenfeld, Wesley Skogan, Jerome Skolnick, Howard Taylor, my anonymous reviewers, the Saint Nicolaas Boat Club of Amsterdam, and all my colleagues at John Jay College of Criminal Justice.

A version of chapter 5 has appeared in *Law Enforcement Executive Forum* 7, no. 4, 137–49, as "911 and the Failure of Police Rapid Response."

CHAPTER 1

The Departed

> Just what I needed, is a college boy. . . . What's your
> degree? . . . Sociology? You'll go far. That's if you
> live. . . . Just don't let your college degree get you killed.
>
> —*Clint Eastwood as Harry Callahan in*
>   Dirty Harry, *1971*

Most days I don't miss being a cop; being a professor is a better job. But I do miss working with people willing to risk their life for me. And as a police officer, I would risk my life for others, even for those I didn't know, and even those I knew I didn't like. That's part of the job. As a professor, my colleagues are great, but there's not a single person at John Jay College of Criminal Justice I would die for. It's not that I wish teaching were more dangerous, but there is something about danger and sweat that makes a beer after work particularly cold and refreshing. You can't learn this in a book.

Danger creates a bond. Most police retire in one piece, and other jobs, at least statistically, are more dangerous. But policing is unique in that injury and death come not just from accidents but from job performance. When a police officer is killed, criminals don't call time out. For police, the show must go on. At a police funeral, no one composes eulogizing platitudes of "never again." It will happen again—just hopefully not to you or anybody you know and love.

The shared experiences of police work help overcome many differences, but the so-called Blue Brotherhood is not a monolithic entity as much as a tent under which a diverse clan of cousins constantly feuds and squabbles. Elite colleges should envy the true racial and economic diversity of an urban police academy. Police identity is not so much a unifying force as a tool that allows effective functioning in spite of differences.[1] As one police academy instructor said, "When you put on that uniform, you're not white or black. You're blue. We're one big happy family, right? Dysfunctional as hell. But what family isn't?"

Police culture is actually less mysterious and exotic than outsiders believe. There is no secret handshake. Social isolation comes not from corruption or brutality but from the grind of daily shift work combined with doses of unfiltered and politically incorrect reality. Being police is working-class and not particularly intellectual. This is more a matter of selection than initiation. Much of what is perceived as police identity—socially conservative values, a rejection of lower-class culture, a resentment and envy of the professional class—is present before officers enter the police department.[2] Many potentially good police are turned off by a shamefully low starting salary, others by the pseudo-military environment of the academy. Standing at attention, saluting, and doing sit-ups are terrible methods to teach the needed police skills of problem-solving, independent thinking, quick action, and the ability to articulate everything. The tricks of the trade involve knowing which corners to cut and why, what form to fill out and how, and when to modulate your radio voice so backup starts heading in your direction before trouble starts.

Fresh out of the academy, police are usually placed in high-crime districts because these areas are the least desirable to work. And besides, you learn fast in the 'hood. You learn about the importunate demands of the dispatcher, the futility of rapid-response, and the persistence and harms of the drug trade. It's unfortunate that the ghetto becomes a real-life training arena. Mistakes are made. High-crime areas are where the best and most experienced patrol officers are needed. The enthusiasm of the young is no substitute for the wisdom of the old. And the on-the-job education of police officers is not all productive. Criminals don't want to work with the police any more than police want to coddle criminals. But when drug laws criminalize so many, the police and public inevitably coexists in barely disguised mutual antipathy. Young police learn that the job has more to do with public control than public service.

Citizens call 911 and expect the police to do something. So police fall back on arrests. And arrest they do. The drug corner is bursting with criminals and addicts seemingly waiting to go to jail. But drug dealers aren't stupid. There are rules of drug dealing that protect most drug dealers. Usually a kid is left holding the bag, literally. The child comes from an overwhelmed and dysfunctional home. The father, very likely, has already been locked up for a drug crime. The child needs many things, but none of these is provided by police. Uniformed police patrol does little but temporarily disrupt public drug dealing.

I know, because for eight and a half hours a night, I policed East Baltimore, one of the worst ghettos in America. "Worst" is a horribly judgmental term. So is "ghetto," for that matter. But in terms of violence, drugs, abandonment, and despair, East Baltimore certainly holds its own. Originally my goal was not to be police officer at all. I was an Ivy League graduate student planning a comparatively mundane one-year study of police socialization. I do not come from a family of police. None of my friends were police. My parents were teachers. I had few dealings with police. I was part of the liberal upper-middle class raised with the kindly lessons of Officer Friendly. As a high-school student, the few times I could have gotten in trouble, Chicago police officers always cut me a break. I'm very polite. And white.

As a sociology graduate student, I took to heart the argument that prolonged participant-observation research is the best and perhaps only means of gathering valid data on job-related police behavior. Because data on policing is iffy at best and cops, like everyone, love to tell a tall tale, the best way to see what happens on the street is to be there as it happens. As an institution, police have been labeled insular, resentful of outsiders, and in general hostile to research, experimentation, and analysis.[3] Official police statistics are notoriously susceptible to manipulation.[4] And as most police activity has no official record at all, the nuances of police work are difficult if not impossible to quantify. Professor and police researcher Maurice Punch wrote, "The researcher's task becomes, then, how to outwit the institutional obstacle-course to gain entry and . . . penetrate the minefield of social defenses to reach the inner reality of police work."[5] I wanted to become an active member of an academy class and follow in the footsteps of M.I.T. professor John Van Maanen, who did this thirty years earlier in Seattle.[6] My plan, after a few rejections from other cities, was accepted in Baltimore, Maryland.[7] I moved to Baltimore knowing the city only from the movies of Barry Levinson and John Waters. I was given a police-officer-trainee uniform and reported at 07:39 hours for day one of the fifth academy class of the year.

On day two, I was pulled out from some mindless military marching drill and told I could not continue as a researcher. The police commissioner who had approved my research, Thomas Frazier, was out. The interim regime was not friendly. Suddenly my research was ex-post disapproved. In a matter of minutes, I was in a very tense meeting with the acting commissioner of the police department. During this rather unpleasant half-hour, he asked me, "Why don't you want to become a cop for real?" Previously I had taken and "passed" the police civil service exam in Massachusetts, but I was never called back.[8] I wondered aloud who would hire me *knowing* I would quit after a year and write a book. He said that he would, if I could meet all the hiring requirements. My research could continue provided I successfully complete an expedited hiring process. I needed to become a fully active and paid police officer.

I passed the battery of tests and ran one and a half miles for the first time in my life. I was hired in two months (a record time) and managed, barely, to stay with my police academy class of "99-5." Meanwhile the acting commissioner was pushed out and Edward Norris from New York City was appointed commissioner. Perhaps I was lost in the shuffle, but I had no further problems continuing my research. As an employee, the research advantages were tremendous. For starters, I was paid.[9] While such pecuniary matters are not supposed to influence objective academic research, a meager paycheck can go a long way to advance the noble pursuit of knowledge, especially since none of my grant applications was accepted.

Going into the academy, I didn't know what to anticipate. As I looked around at my classmates, I thought, "I may not be the best cop in here, but I certainly won't be the worst." I thought I could handle the job, but not because

I knew what to expect. I'm good at improvising. And even if policing isn't the best job, there are certainly worse.

On the street, new police officers learn quickly because they have to. And what do they learn? That they're to patrol in their cars, respond to 911 and 311 calls for service, take reports, and make arrests by sending drug users and sellers through the justice system's revolving-door. Police officers learn that they're on the streets to serve the needs of the larger war—and to make it look like the battles are being won. Over time, the connections between the war on drugs and the demands placed on police officers became crystal clear. Police attack drug corners as if they were brush fires, stomping out one only to see it flare up again as soon as they move on to the next. People's desire to get high and a stubborn national commitment to drug prohibition provide the fuel. Drug dealers and users are just the kindling. As police can not get at the source, they do what police do best: lock people up. Our nation's poorest and least wanted are swept off the streets, sorted by the courts, and collected in our jails and prisons. But sooner or later they all come back, ready to burn again.[10]

Some will criticize my unscientific methods. I have no real defense. Everything is true, but this book suffers from all the flaws inherent in ethnographic work and some, perhaps, of gonzo journalism.[11] Being on the inside, I made little attempt to be objective. I did not pick, much less randomly pick, my research site or research subjects. I researched where I was assigned. To those I policed, I tried to be fair. But my empathy was toward my fellow officers. Those next to me became my friends and research subjects. My theories emerged from experience, knowledge, and understanding. In academic jargon, my work could be called "front- and backstage, multisited, participant-observation research using grounded theory rooted in symbolic interactionism from a dramaturgical perspective." But I can't even say it with a straight face. And if I wrote that way, very few would read it.

My notes varied greatly in both quality and quantity. Ultimately they filled about 350 single-spaced, typed pages. But I should have typed more. Some days I felt I had nothing to say. Other days I had a lot to say but was too tired to say it. After a long night's work and a few beers, it was too easy to convince myself that memory would suffice. Whatever I didn't write down is gone forever. Just one example: on May 28, 2001, I helped guard the crime scene of a twelve-person shooting. I remember being there, talking and whiling the night away, making tasteless jokes about the blood-spattered remains of the food spread. Out of boredom, I smoked a cigar another officer gave to me. I don't even like cigars. Six years later, when I looked back to my notes, the entry for the night was blank. Perhaps I had nothing insightful to say. It's still more likely that I thought I would never forget the details of a twelve-person shooting. Well, I have.

Most police officers—whether out of a desire to express themselves or the simple boredom of being confined in the intimate space of a squad car for eight hours—speak extremely candidly. Usually I would talk to my squadmates parked next to me in the classic police style: driver's-side window adjacent to driver's-side window. Undoubtedly my greatest sources were those with whom I became friends. Given time, I had the luxury of being able to wait for sensitive issues to come up naturally. When such topics arose (or when I could bring them up), I would ask extremely pointed and personal questions. More often than not, I could spark candid conversations. Except when noted, all quotations come from personal conversations with police officers, mostly my squadmates.

As a group, police officers are not inclined toward heady discussions of academic theory. Like everybody, police officers talk about personal relationships, sports, hobbies, and plans for days off. Perhaps more unique to police, conversations frequently veer toward the sick humor of the most recent call-for-service; ineptitude in the police organization; and sexual matters true, false, and fantasized. In the day-to-day routine, the inner working of a big-city police department resembles a bureaucratic Kafkaesque nightmare more than the latest installment of *C.S.I.: Crime Scene Investigation*.

When taking notes for a book, it helps that pen and paper are required for police officers. Usually I jotted a few things at the scene and expanded my writing when I returned home from work. I reconstructed quotes as quickly as possible and to the best of my memory. I experimented with, and then decided against, tape recording police interviews. Data from recorded interviews were less revealing than what I could gather through casual conversation. While accurate transcripts are extremely useful for quotes, I found that when the tape recorder is running, police officers remain on-guard, talking in a stilted and formal style reminiscent of police officers on the TV show *Cops*. (I loved the show *Cops* before I was a cop. But as a police officer I learned to dislike it. Partly I didn't want to watch work videos when I wasn't working. And without a doubt, police conversations are far more revealing when the camera isn't rolling. But even more than that, I don't like watching bad policing. To the outsider, good policing should appear boring. It is only when things go wrong and mistakes are made that policing becomes entertainment.) A few times I brought a small laptop computer and could write detailed notes during slow periods on the midnight shift. But the steering wheel gets in the way of the screen.

Because of the nature of the work and the cultural background of most police officers, language is very sexual, scatological, and personal. The concept of "political correctness" is simultaneously understood and mocked. One officer said, "[People in the Eastern District are] drugged-out, lazy motherfuckers. These people don't want to work. They want to sit on their ass, collect welfare, get drunk, and make babies. Let them shoot each other." After a brief pause he turned to me and said with faux sincerity, "I think the problems here are caused by social conditions, which can be solved by better education. . . . That's so when you write down all this stuff for your book I don't come out like an asshole." While quotes selected naturally emphasize the extreme over the mundane, I believe they represent the collective views of most police officers I worked with.

I never intended to write a "kiss-and-tell." There's better kissing-and-telling out there.[12] The only real scandals I saw were living conditions in the ghetto and a general lack of support for hard-working police officers. There is no culture of corruption or brutality among Baltimore City patrol officers. Police love *talking* about beatings, but I did not see any police commit criminal acts. Good behavior, while not universal, is the norm. This is not to say that police, myself included, are angels. Police violate departmental regulations all the time. Like any other public employee with bad working conditions, obnoxious customers, and excellent job security, police get pissed off and can be assholes. I tried not to be.

I happily worked midnights, generally the least desirable shift. I've always been a night owl. Unlike day police work, midnight shifts usually quiet down after a few unrelenting hours. Other officers like midnights because of steady work hours, faster commutes, an almost nonexistent upper-management presence, and less conflict with daytime family or work responsibilities.

I wasn't a police officer for long, just six months in the academy and fourteen months on the street. But you learn quickly on the streets of the Eastern District. As one veteran police dispatcher said, "You handle more kinds of calls by the end of field training than other cops handle in their careers." With less than two weeks on the street, I was the primary officer responding to a shooting. Officers with thirty years in a safe suburb might wonder if they can handle East Baltimore. My squadmates and I know we can handle anything. Given my short tenure, early on I decided not to seek a transfer within the department. I knew I could never know the entire police organization. I wanted to learn one part very well. Plus, I had a good sergeant.

The Eastern District is one of nine police districts in Baltime City. Roughly the boundaries are E. 25th Street and Sinclair Lane on the north, Orleans Street and Pulaski Highway on the south, Fallsway on the west, and Erdman Avenue on the east. Landmarks include Johns Hopkins Hospital, Dunbar High School (home of the Poets), the Old-Town Mall, the North-East Market, and the National Great Blacks in Wax Museum. I generally policed the middle of the district, straddling Broadway from Orleans to

North Ave. The area suffers from crime, drugs, and blight. Ninety-seven percent of the district is African American. The poverty rate is 37 percent. Once a working-class area with a variety of ethnic groups, the district lost most of its population, first through white flight and then through working-class black flight. The 2000 Census counted 45,081 residents, almost one-third less than in 1990.[13]

The Eastern District police station, under the command of a major, has about 260 police officers. Approximately half the officers are assigned to uniformed patrol. Each eight-and-a-half-hour patrol shift has about forty uniformed officers, three sergeants, and one lieutenant. A patrol sergeant is in charge of a squad of twelve to fourteen officers, five to eight of whom are working on any given day. Every squad is permanently assigned to one of the district's three sectors, which is further divided geographically into four to six "posts" (i.e., beats). Though posts vary greatly in size throughout the city, all fourteen posts in the Eastern District are small geographic areas (thirty-five to 100 small city blocks) containing 3,000 to 6,000 residents. When a squad has enough working officers and functioning police cars, one or two officers will be assigned to work one post.

A squad is expected to collectively handle all the calls within its sector. Ideally post officers handle all the calls on their post. But officers are routinely assigned to any call in their sector. While officers typically do not work outside their squad or police outside their sector, the three squads of the Eastern District go to the same roll call and are on the same radio frequency. Being on the same frequency, officers will assist others as appropriate. Except for a "Signal-13," a call to help an officer in trouble, policing outside one's district is extremely rare. Unlike some cities and all police TV shows and movies, Baltimore police usually patrol solo, without a partner.

Though almost all names have been changed in this book, pseudonyms aren't enough to guarantee anonymity for those familiar with the people involved. Not only is the protection of individuals who trusted me an institutional requirement, it is also a matter of common courtesy. Personal identifiers, although always accurate, are intentionally vague and not always consistent. A "female instructor" in one chapter may be a "black sergeant" in another chapter. My squadmates can likely attribute many quotes based on style of speech. But my goal is to allow plausible deniability. I am less protective of those who have retired and given me permission to quote them. Characters, as a nonfiction literary device, are kept to a minimum. Admittedly the results—disjointed, sensational, out-of-context quotations—are a handicap to writer and reader alike. Such sacrifices are necessary for the approval of universities' Human Subjects' Committees. Much research suffers when academics are prevented from observing and conversing like a normal free person.

Beyond the obvious nature of administering questionnaires, I would not mention my research status unprompted. One does not endear oneself to police with talk of one's privileged, educational background. But word of me spread vaguely through the grapevine. When the subject of my research came up in groups, others often described me as "writing a book." This usually proved an adequate answer. I would sometimes add that I was writing a book on policing in general and not police officers in particular. More often than not, sociology was confused with social work or psychology. When questioned, I tried to explain my research goals as clearly as possible, a task made difficult by the fact I really had no clear research goals.

On the street, my squadmates were at first suspicious about my literary intentions. Initially my presence was greeted with skepticism, especially from supervisors who believed, probably accurately, that nothing good could come from my writing. One lieutenant told me: "Moskos, I like you. But I don't want anything to do with your book. I don't want to be in it. I don't want my name in it. I don't want any part of it." Outside of this reference, he's not. Another officer asked me rhetorically, "You know how many times people have come up to me and asked, 'What's with the Harvard guy? What's he doing here?'" But police officers are primarily concerned with staying safe, staying out of trouble, and not jeopardizing their pensions. Policing is certainly a job like no other. But by and large for most police—day in and day out and for better and for worse—the job is just a job.

By doing my job, being personable, and drinking after work, I was accepted for who I was: a police officer using the department as a stepping stone to something better. This stepping-stone attitude was encouraged by many officers. Ultimately I felt I was judged as all police are: work performance and personality. On the street I received no hazing and had no problem receiving backup. As far as I know, coworkers did not mind riding with me as a partner. Police officers wished me luck on my book and urged me not to forget them. I haven't.

Toward the end of my time I could ask about my acceptance, especially during the early period. I was told by a squadmate, "Before you got here [in our squad], Sarge said to watch out: 'He's writing a friggin' book! He's going to put all our names in it and give it to I.I.D. [Internal Affairs]!' I told Sarge you were going to change all the names." The wife of my sergeant confirmed this, "I'll never forget when [he] came home and said he had some guy writing a book or something. He doesn't like to admit it now, but he told the whole squad to watch themselves when you were around. Because who knows what you would say." My sergeant added, "I didn't know who you were or what your motives were." I asked him why he would be so worried since nothing really bad was going on. He gave me a tired and quizzical look before saying, "It depends on how you define 'bad.'" One partner told me, "Everyone said I should watch out. But I didn't think that. I just wanted to know if you were going to do your job." Another officer was more blunt, "I don't care what you're going to write. What's the worst you're going to say? That I sleep on the job? Oh well. Yeah, I do and so do you." On a quiet midnight shift, who doesn't?

Certainly, as in any situation, I was accepted by some more than others. While writing a book wasn't a problem per se, being college-educated and politically liberal did affect some people's attitude toward me. In the police station one young, conservative, white police officer asked me, "How can you be a cop and be a liberal? . . . Oh that's right, you're not a cop, you're just here to get your PhD." In the academy one instructor confronted me by saying, "You're probably one of those smart cops who hangs in those fancy coffee shops wired to the Internet. [You] think you're too good for Dunkin' Donuts!"

At times, colleagues went out of the way to help my data collection. One African American colleague proposed a working title for my book: "The Pits of Hell of East Baltimore."

The same officer got on the radio once to announce a foot chase. After the dispatcher's repeated prompting, it became obvious that the officer, panting and exhausted, had no clue where he was. Finally, between gasps for breath, the officer earnestly responded with a description so useless it was hilarious: "I'm in an alley, it's dark, and there's a lot of trash." A colleague wrote this down and gave it to me later so it wouldn't be forgotten.

My work style, influenced by my aversion to court, was not to go out seeking adventure or arrests. I saw my strengths in dealing well with people, calming situations, and writing good reports. As my sergeant put it, "Pete's not a fireball on the street, but he's got his act together." My arrest totals—between zero and eight per month—were less than many rookies but more than most veterans. I could handle action but looked forward to slow nights. Bad weather keeps people inside and the radio quiet. I was more than happy to get paid to read the newspaper. My primary goal, like most police officers, was to return home safely every day.

Living in Baltimore City, I was required to carry my gun both on and off duty. I never fired a shot outside of training. Only rarely was my service weapon—a charged semiautomatic nine-millimeter Glock-17 with no safety and a seventeen-round clip—pointed at somebody.[14] But in my police duties, my gun was very routinely removed from its holster, probably every other shift. I did occasionally chase people down alleys and wrestled a few suspects. I maced one person, but did not hit anybody. As a police officer, I tried to speak softly and carry a big stick. The department issued a twenty-nine-inch straight wooden baton just for this purpose. I brought it along to all my calls.

In any account of police work, inevitably the noncriminal public, the routine, and the working folks all get short shrift. Police don't deal with a random cross-section of society, even within the areas they work. And this book reflects that. The ghetto transcends stereotypes. Families try to make it against the odds. Old women sweep the streets. People rise before dawn to go to work. On Sundays, ladies go to church wearing beautiful hats and preachers preach to the choir. But if you're looking for stereotypes, they're there. Between the vacant and abandoned buildings you'll find liquor stores, fast food, Korean corner stores, and a Jewish pawn shop. Living conditions are worse than third-world shanty towns: children in filthy apartments without plumbing or electricity, entire homes put out on eviction day, forty-five-year-old great-grand parents, junkies not raising their kids, drug dealers, and everywhere signs of violence and despair.

As a middle-class white man policing the ghetto, I should address the charge of "exoticism," that I use poor residents for my own advantage.[15] I plead no-contest. If you're not from the ghetto, and though it may not be politically correct to say so, the ghetto *is* exotic. One field-training officer accused me of being "*fascinated* by the ghetto." I am. There are very few aspects of urban life that don't fascinate me. But it is not my intent to sensationalize the ghetto. This is a book about police.

If you want to read about the ghetto, good books are out there.[16] Ghettos are diverse and encompass many cultures and classes. Some object to the very term ghetto. I use the word because it is the vernacular of police officers and many (though by no means all) of the residents. If you really want to learn about the ghetto, go there. There's probably one near you. Visit a church; walk down the street; buy something from the corner store; have a beer; eat. But most importantly, talk to people. That's how you learn. When the subject turns to drugs and crime, you'll hear a common refrain: "It just don't make sense."

Twenty months in Baltimore wasn't very long, but it was long enough to see five police officers killed in the line of duty. And there were other cops, friends of mine, who were hurt, shot, and lucky to live. A year after I quit the force, my friend and academy classmate became the first Baltimore police woman killed in the line of duty, dying in a car crash on the way to backup another police officer.

Crystal Sheffield patrolled opposite me in the Western District. Occasionally I would switch my radio over to the Western District channel to see what she was up to. When she died, I returned to Baltimore, hitched a ride in a police car from the train station to the funeral, and stood in the cold rain at attention in my civilian clothes with my uniformed fellow officers. Police funerals are one of the few events that bring together law enforcement. Funerals give meaning to that often clichéd concept of Blue Brotherhood. At an officer's funeral, police-car lights flash as far as the eye can see. Thousands of police officers wearing white gloves and black bands on their badges stand at attention. Guns are fired in salute. Bagpipes are played. A flag is folded. The coffin is lowered into the ground.

At the end of a police funeral, a dispatcher from headquarters calls for the fallen officer over all radio channels. The response, of course, is silence. After the third attempt the dispatcher states the officer is "10-7." Ten-seven is the rather unsentimental radio code for "out of service." Ten-seven usually refers to a car, an officer handling a call, or an anonymous murder victim on the street. To hear your friend and colleague described as 10-7 is heartbreaking. In this way the few officers left working the streets know the burial is complete.

A few seconds later a routine drug call is dispatched or one bold officer reclaims the radio airwaves for some mundane police matter. A car stop. A warrant check. A request for a case number. The show goes on. *Sometimes it just don't make sense.*

CHAPTER 2

Back to School:
The Police Academy

Do you find yourself being slowly sucked
into the oppressive right-wing conspiracy?

—*Eastern District sergeant to the author*

Just before I started the Baltimore police academy, as
I unceremoniously collected my first installment of
police uniform and equipment in two large black plastic
garbage bags, one quartermaster officer warned me that everything I would learn in the academy is "bullshit."[1] The
second officer at the quartermasters said it was a shame to
see kids raised by parents who couldn't raise them, with
chicken bones and garbage all over the house, and have it
all paid for by the taxpayer. He said, "I don't want to name
any 'nationalities,' you can figure out what I'm talking
about." "You ain't going to change them," the first said.
"Just make sure they don't change you," I responded. Both
officers were older white men and very burned out. I wondered what they had done to end up working in the win-
dowless basement of police headquarters.

Such was my introduction to the police academy. For those
visiting Baltimore, the police academy can be associated with
the amusing sight of pained trainees chanting politically correct cadence while jogging in formation through the Inner
Harbor. Yet even the blandest cadence (Everywhere we go/
People want to know/Who we are/So we tell them/We're
the P.D./The mighty mighty P.D./The Baltimore P.D.)

inspired one black man to shout "murderers" during the pause between lines. While military formation may give the impression of a disciplined organization transforming recruits into well trained professionals, the 1988 screwball comedy *Police Academy*, while not exactly realistic, may be more truthful. Mostly trainees sit in stuffy and run-down classrooms, do push-ups, and passively get pushed through a six-month, state-accredited police training program.

The day starts with 7:30 AM uniform inspection. Superiors are addressed as "sir" and "ma'am." Orders are to be strictly followed. The academy class stands at attention when any police officer or instructor enters or exits a classroom. The majority of instructors are police officers. Trainees learn both the strict, military-inspired "chain of command" and their low status in this chain. Real and perceived violations of rules are punished—"rewarded" in academy parlance—by push-ups and other forms of physical exercise. Trainees are not allowed to leave the floor of the building on their own initiative at any point during the day. The police academy, despite its pedagogical ideals, is considered work rather than school. Unlike some police academies (particularly state police agencies), Baltimore trainees do not live on campus.

Police academy trainees do not have police powers but are fully paid employees of the police department. Trainees are distinguished from full police officers because they wear khaki pants with a police shirt and do not carry a gun. After completing the police academy program, the police officer trainee is granted the power of arrest and the obligation to carry a gun. But six months in the academy tells the police officer very little about how police work is done and much about the dysfunctional nature of a big-city police department.

The academy is more like the world's worst all-inclusive vacation than a finely tuned training machine. On most days, trainees would be "rewarded" with between 50 and 200 push-ups, usually issued in units of ten or twenty-five push-ups. Trainees would count push-ups by proclaiming, "One, sir; two, sir; three, sir . . ." or "ma'am" as appropriate. Leg lifts and other forms of calisthenics were punishment for such activities as talking in class, gum chewing, failing certain questions, and falling asleep. Often the class was punished for unknown reasons and perhaps no reason at all.

In one day spent learning self-defense and baton techniques, various instructors spent a combined total of two hours verbally berating and belittling the class. In a typical barrage, one instructor yelled at the class, "You have no rights! If you think I can't fire you, you're wrong. That's what we have these 95s [written records of misbehavior] for. And I have a huge stack from this class. Nobody can protect you, not the FOP [Fraternal Order of Police], not your lawyer, not your mama." Soon, however, the class saw these repeated threats of job termination were seen as the hollow threats they were. The academy is not a "weed-out" process. The academy environment is less a learning process than a ritualized hazing to be endured. Except for one trainee held back due to injury, all members of the academy graduated on time and became police officers.[2]

Seemingly oblivious to the reality shock that trainees would face once they hit the streets, the academy did its best to separate trainees from active police officers. Active patrol officers were generally seen by higher ups not as mentors but as tainted and potentially corrupting influences.[3] By the end of the academy, fully a quarter of police officers saw the police organization as hindering police work, twice the percentage found at the beginning of the police academy.[4] Baltimore police trainees learned more about surviving in a dysfunctional organization—low standards, leaky roofs, shortages of paper and forms, arbitrary punishment—than about policing the community.

So what's the point of the academy? The first is to protect the department from the legal liability that could result from negligent training. To the trainees this appears more important than educating police officers. As one trainee said, "They're not doing it to protect our ass, they're doing it to cover theirs." It was important to meet the Maryland mandated 502 training objectives, so classes were taught to the tests. If that wasn't enough, there was an open secret that answers to some tests would be given to the class in pretest "review sessions." And second, despite the lax approach toward academics, instructors were very concerned with officer safety, the aspect of the job they emphasized most: "The most important part of your job is that you go home. Everything else is secondary." This philosophy is reinforced at all levels of the police organization. Formal and informal rules concerning officer safety are propagated simultaneously.

One class showed videos from Fox TV shows of cops getting attacked or killed. Most involved discretionary attempts by police officers to search cars for drugs. The instructor warned the class, "Do you ever think that this could happen? That this could happen in Maryland? That this could happen in Baltimore? That someone in this class

may be killed? This is no joke. . . . We're teaching you survival techniques. You're going to the 'hood." Police officers
learn and generally follow legal rules of use of force. Police
officers are not allowed to shoot except for the immediate
preservation of life. A police officer gave the class very wise
advice: "Your goal, as is my goal, is to lead a boring life."
There are departmentally approved self-defense techniques,
but when it comes to survival, anything goes. As the movie
Departed put it: "Cop. . . . Criminal. . . . When you're facing a loaded gun, what does it matter?"

Police academy classes cover subjects such as report writing, law, and physical training. My academy class boasted
fifty trainees, none of whom admitted to being challenged
by any of the class material outside of law class. Academy
instruction varied greatly in terms of quality. Deserving of
praise were the classes in law, shooting, and driving. Law
class was graced with two excellent instructors, one a lawyer and the other a police officer. The shooting and driving
instructions took place at separate locations and, like law,
were distinguished by instructors who cared about the subject matter and demonstrated a sincere desire to pass their
knowledge on to the trainees.

And although many police-officer instructors were dedicated, others couldn't teach and seemed motivated primarily
by the academy's regular Monday-to-Friday, 8-AM-to-4-PM
schedule, a rarity in the police department. Most civilian instructors were even worse, ranging from out-of-touch to
completely ignorant. Overall there was little emphasis on
subject retention. In the academy, very little attempt was
made to relate class material to actual police work. Routine
activities such as filling out practice forms and learning

10-codes wasted a lot of time. These would be better and much more quickly learned on the street.

By the end of the academy, less than half the class saw a relation between what police learn in the academy and what police need to know on the street.[5] A strong antimedia attitude, little changed from sociologist William Westley's observations in the 1950s, grew steadily in the police academy.[6] At the end of training, just 10 percent of trainees believed that the media treat police fairly. Notably, after trainees spent a year on the street, this percentage increased slightly, to 15 percent.

The best lesson of the police academy was told to us on the first day of the police academy: "When in doubt, shut your mouth and look sharp!" After six months in the academy, trainees learn to:

- Respect the chain of command and your place on the bottom of that chain.
- Sprinkle "sir" and "ma'am" into casual conversation.
- Salute.
- Follow orders.
- March in formation.
- Stay out of trouble.
- Stay awake.
- Be on time.
- Shine shoes.

All in all, these aren't horrible lessons for life, and they even come in handy for a smattering of police work: being assigned to boring details, major emergency situations, police funerals, and when filmed by TV news. But these lessons could be taught in one week and are horribly inappropriate for the bulk of day-to-day police work. That police organizations continue to perpetuate a myth of quasimilitary professionalism shows an institutional conservative bias and a justifiable insecurity in the department's ability to control the rank-and-file.[7]

A system dependent on supervisory presence, responsibility, and control cannot succeed in a day-to-day work environment in which supervisors are not present. A police officer can follow orders until his or her first solo call for service when, very suddenly, there is no boss or colleague to ask for advice. Police patrol demands lessons wholly lacking in the police academy: bold, independent, intelligent, and thoughtful actions. Decisions need to be made and made quickly. Troubled people need to be told what to do and listened to. All this in an environment where people don't respect authority, don't want to be told what to do, and don't give a damn about any quasimilitary chain of command. We have no choice but to trust police officers and hold them responsible for their actions. The fact that most manage so well in a system designed to restrain them is a credit to police officers' ingenuity and dedication.[8]

Police departments typically codify proper rules in shockingly great and verbose detail. The Baltimore Police Department's book of General Orders, without index or page numbers, comes in at a binder-bursting five-inches thick. Violations of any code can be grounds for disciplinary action. Any deviation from the proper rules—no matter how smart, creative, and well intentioned—is potentially subject to departmental disciplinary action.[9] Yet some violations of the book of general orders are so engrained as to be standard operating procedure. Understood is that the efficiency of the informal rules allows the formal rules to survive.

Though faced in all occupations, the gap between how things *must* be done (the formal rules) and how things *should* be done (the informal rules that develop over time) is larger and more critical in policing. The relationship between formal and informal rules is simultaneously schizophrenic and symbiotic. Two researchers who studied the role of formal rules in police departments put it this way:

> Police officers who avoid or evade [formal rules] are considered as deviants, actors who deviate from the proper. Deviants, contrary to public opinion, sometimes make positive contributions to the success and vitality of organizations. . . . Such deviant behavior sometimes is copied by actors who have important positions in the organization. As other actors join the bandwagon, [a "smarter," informal rule] slowly develops.[10]

Many instructors in the police academy emphasized the formal rules of policing by proudly, but uselessly, stating variations of: "There are two ways of doing things: a wrong way and a right way!" One more thoughtful sergeant addressed the tension between the formal and informal rules. He told me that, "There's a lot of gray [in policing]. Too many cops think there's right and wrong. Good guys and bad. You've got to accept the gray and deal with it." Most instructors studiously ignored this gray zone.

When faced with the obvious conflict between the formal ideal and informal reality of departmental rules, some instructors would roll their eyes at times and say things such as, "This is what they want me to teach, but you'll see how things are done soon enough." In a class on the department's vehicle pursuit policy, the instructor lectured, reading in monotone from his notes: "The pursuit policy, which is General Order O3, states that pursuits are only to be done in exigent circumstances, when immediate action is necessary, and when there is no alternative, and when failure to pursue would likely cause grave accident or death. The general order also states that a police car may under no circumstances ever drive more than ten miles per hour over the posted speed limit. *[Pause]* Everybody knows this is a joke, but I just have to teach you what the General Orders say."

The same instructor later offered the class a bit of informal advice. In response to a question about chasing cars he stated, "You can't chase a car. It's not allowed. I've never *'chased'* a car." But then he added with a mischievous smile, "But I've *'followed'* a few."

The formal versus informal rules are most obvious when it comes to the war on drugs. There is no local residency requirement for Baltimore police officers, and only a minority of trainees had any experience with any of the high-drug areas within the city. Most police officers have little prior experience with illegal drugs. Police officers are randomly tested for drug use and numerous unannounced urine tests were administered during the course of the hiring process and in the police academy. Any admission of frequent or recent illegal drug use in one's private life would prevent an applicant from being hired. It should be noted that with a little learning, lying and passing a polygraph exam, the lie detector test, is not a difficult skill to master. Likewise telling the truth in no way guarantees passing this flawed test. Numerous trainees, myself included, admitted in private conversations that they successfully deceived the polygrapher and lied on the lie detector test.

Informally many more than the official twenty hours of instruction in the police academy were dedicated to the topic of drugs. Instructors warned the class about the severity of Baltimore's drug problems.[11] One sergeant said, "You'll be surprised. You all don't know anything. This drug thing is out of control." Trainees are told that 80 to 85 percent of Baltimore homicides are drug-related and an equal percentage of calls for service are related to drugs. With a broad definition of "drug related," both figures are in the ballpark.

Some of the formal distinctions learned in the academy were both useful and important on the street. A class member used the phrase "frisking for drugs." The police officer instructor responded: "No, no, no, no, no, no, no! You don't frisk for drugs, only for weapons. And then only for officer safety. . . . You'll see veteran officers do that all the time. Don't fall for it. It's a VCR search-and-frisk—violation of constitutional rights." Expanding on the theme of constitutional rights, an African American instructor said: "You can't just go up to someone and put your hands on them. People have died for their civil rights. And don't you think it's ironic that you, sworn to uphold laws and the constitution, would go and violate the constitution? I mean, you have to look inside yourself and ask why you're here." An officer on the street implied that illegal behavior just sort of sneaks up on you: "Nobody goes out there *wanting* to violate rights."

Police power is limited by the U.S. Constitution. Though written decades before the first municipal police force, the Fourth Amendment of the Bill of Rights defines the legal standards police need to stop, search, and arrest a criminal suspect: "The right of the people to be secure in their persons, houses, papers, and effects, against unreasonable searches and seizures, shall not be violated, and no warrants shall issue, but upon probable cause, supported by oath or affirmation, and particularly describing the place to be searched, and the persons or things to be seized." While a logical reading of the Fourth Amendment would imply that a person cannot be searched or seized without a warrant supported by probable cause, the courts have determined that warrantless searches and arrests are permissible in many circumstances.[12] Warrantless arrests far outnumber suspects brought in on an arrest warrant. Because of the Fourth Amendment, police officers must have "probable cause" for every search or arrest. After an arrest, the judicial branch (in Baltimore, a representative from the Office of State's Attorney) accepts or rejects the officer's written statement of probable cause. Usually probable cause is granted, but if, in the opinion of the judicial branch, probable cause is not met, the suspect is released immediately.

The courts have further distinguished between an arrest and the "stop" that usually precedes a warrantless arrest. A stop is defined as when a person cannot or does not feel free to leave. Only "reasonable suspicion" is needed for a stop. The definition of reasonable suspicion varies somewhat, but it is often defined as less than probable cause, more than a hunch, and, in more legal phrasing, dependent on the totality of the circumstances and the articulable knowledge of the officer involved. This creates an interesting situation where a suspect could be legally stopped by one police officer but this same stop by the police officer's partner could be illegal.

The legality of a stop or search does not depend on the actions of the suspect as much as the ability of police officers to articulate the legal standards needed to justify their actions. An officer could *tell* a suspect, "Come here," or *ask* the suspect, "Do you mind coming over here?" The ability to use and then write the latter is the difference between a potential conviction and an illegal stop. The legal difference between the imperative and the "request" determines the exact moment at which a "stop" occurred. Knowledge of a suspect's prior criminal history, physical movement on the part of a suspect consistent with drug or gun possession, working in a violent or high-drug area, and an officer's level of fear can all be used to articulate reasonable suspicion and justify a police stop and frisk of a suspect.

The 1968 Supreme Court Case *Terry v. Ohio* gives officers the right to frisk a suspect for weapons if they have reasonable suspicion that a suspect might be armed. A "Terry Frisk" is a limited pat down of the outer clothing for weapons. This is distinct from and less than a "search" (for which probable cause is needed). While a limited pat down of the outer clothing for weapons may seem benign, a frisk is very personal and intrusive. During any encounter, an officer can justify a frisk of a suspect by noting the drug trade in the area and the inherent link between drugs and violence. Legality depends on an officer's perception of his or her own safety. And given the violence, officers in some neighborhoods have good reason to fear for their safety.

The result of *Terry v. Ohio* is a huge legal loophole in which people in high-crime neighborhoods, usually young black men, are stopped and frisked far more often than people in other neighborhoods. Intended or not, constitutional rights depend on the neighborhood where you live. While race blind in theory, the Terry Frisk (confusingly also known as a Terry Stop or Terry Search), gives police the legal right to stop and frisk *most* individuals in a violent, high-drug area. Technically a Terry Frisk may be used only to find weapons. But any contraband in plain view or "plain feel" is fair game, even if the found object was not the original goal. While reaching into someone's pockets is technically and legally a search, one can easily feel drugs from outside a pocked while ostensibly frisking for weapons.

In the police academy, trainees are instructed how to use the Terry Frisk to make drug lock-ups. If drugs are found on a suspect during a frisk for weapons, officers should complete their search for weapons before addressing the issue of the suspected drugs. If a police officer were to stop a frisk for weapons upon finding drugs, it would be obvious— since drugs are not a direct threat to a police officer's safety—that the intention of the search was not really officer safety. Once hands go in pockets, a legal frisk becomes an illegal search. The Terry Frisk explicitly does *not* give police the right to search or empty pockets. But on the street the line between a frisk and a search is not as clear cut as the Supreme Court wants to believe. Necessary as the Terry Frisk is, in the war on drugs, officers on the street commonly exploit and abuse *Terry v. Ohio.*

After an arrest, for everybody's safety, suspects and their surrounding area are searched in what is known as "search incident to arrest." If the arrested person was driving, the vehicle will be searched before being towed. This is technically required for the "inventory and safekeeping of personal property." But in reality, vehicle searches are more commonly used to find drugs or other contraband. In Baltimore, an arrested prisoner is then strip searched in Baltimore's state-run city jail (Central Booking and Intake Center, referred to by its former acronym C.B.I.F.).

Many people—usually out-of-town white people—are shocked and offended when required to strip after being arrested for some "minor offense." While a strip search is inherently degrading. Prisoners need to keep in mind that while they may not like being strip searched, it really is better than everybody else in jail has been strip searched. There are many very violent people arrested in Baltimore. Despite the fact that suspects have been searched twice before entering C.B.I.F.—once by the arresting officer and again by the wagon officer transporting the prisoner—it is rare but not uncommon to find weapons only during the strip search. It is more common to find drugs.

Our academy class was supposed to visit Central Booking, but for some reason unclear to me, while walking to the jail, someone denied us permission to enter the state-run facility. The class turned back and the visit was never rescheduled. More successful was the de rigueur trip to the morgue. I doubt anybody forgets their first autopsy. The morgue's proper title is the Office of the Chief Medical Examiner. We had been warned by a visitor from the office, "If you want to have good relations with us, don't call us the morgue or the coroner." Medical examiners are doctors and conduct about 4,000 autopsies annually in Baltimore.

While at the time the visit to the morgue seemed primarily designed to shock and awe, in hindsight, it provided a necessary introduction to the fragility of the human body. Familiarity and gallows humor are two effective tools to deal with the gore, mangled bodies, and violent deaths police see on the street. Visitors first see a little slide show about the office's history, rigor mortis, and a few gory pictures. The building also houses "The Nutshell Studies of

Unexplained Death," a fascinating collection of 1940s doll-house crime scenes.

The actual slicing and dicing happens in the basement examination room, which looks like a cross between an operating room and a kitchen, complete with sinks and cutting boards. Above each table is an electrical outlet box and an apparatus that resembled the thing Jiffy Lube uses to put oil in your car. As one officer put it, "This is a sick building." About eight stretchers were laid out with dead bodies: a gun-shot victim, a jail-cell suicide, a guy on a bike hit by a car. There was a smell, not of human decomposition (we were lucky that day), but more like the bloody smell of a good meat market. Except, of course, this was human meat.

The tone in the examination room is more matter-of-fact than reverential. In a standard autopsy, assistants open the chest, cut through the fat and ribs with a little hand-held circular saw, pull out all the organs, weigh the organs, and stuff the organs back in. They also pull the skin of the head over the face to get in the brain. In an image I can't shake from my memory, a bit of discharge came out of a dead man's penis as one worker reached inside the corpse's bowels, perhaps in contact with the seminal vesicle. I'm not certain why anybody would want to work in the morgue, assistants don't make a lot of money. But it's a job that somebody has got to do.

Despite the formal aspirations of the police academy, the best lessons were often learned in more informal settings outside the building. Some previous academy classes had visited the Holocaust Museum in Washington, DC, learning about the potential abuse of state and police power. Our class did not take this field trip. Yet the question of police identity, and the transformation from civilian to police, was never far the thoughts of trainees. One classmate began to walk with a wide-armed police swagger before the wearing of the equipment-laden utility belts necessitated such a stride. Another trainee asked in class if there was a secret handshake for police. He may have been joking. But the rest of the class was curious: How *do* police tell police from nonpolice? How do you know if a car you pull over is driven by a police officer? If you're off-duty and have to pull a gun on a suspect, how do you tell the responding officers that you're a police officer? Fraternal Order of Police and Police Benevolent Association key chains and stickers aren't worth much.

For the record, there is no secret police handshake. Of course some cops have the stereotypical cop look: hair short on the sides, sunglasses, and white officers seem partial to moustaches. If police don't have very good posture, they often suffer from the aches and pains of a sedentary lifestyle combined with a heavy utility belt. Some police talk like cops, with a military bearing (especially those with a military background) and the quick use of sir and ma'am. But as police departments become more diverse, the "cop look" and "cop behavior" becomes less and less indicative. Even police badges are largely for show as they can be bought on eBay, and there is no shortage of police impersonators. "Credentials," a police-issued photo-ID card, are less collectable and offer better verification. Locally police tend to use informal knowledge. Every officer in Baltimore has a sequence or "short" number, a letter followed by three numbers. This is not the badge number, as badges can be lost or stolen. The short number is both a permanent identifier and has the added benefit of dating you. Each letter represents 1,000 hired officers and serves as a generational marker. I was G-556. My sergeant was a D. I even worked with a B; he had thirty-three years on the force. In 2007, officers talk with disdain about the latest I-series officers.

As a Baltimore police officer, I couldn't pass as a New York City cop because I can't speak the local lingo. While policing is fundamentally the same in different cities, there are many linguistic differences between locales. In radio communications, most police use a formal system of 10-codes. A few 10-codes are nearly universal: 10-4 always means OK, 10-7 is out of service, 10-6 is usually stand by, and 10-13 often means some form of officer in trouble. But in Baltimore there is no 10-13. An officer in major trouble is a Signal 13. 10-20 is almost always location, but in New York City it means a robbery not in-progress. This Tower of Babel becomes a problem when police from different jurisdictions respond to a common disaster. Lack of communication is one problem, but more dangerous are misinterpretations of the same 10-code.

There is a growing movement to do away with 10-codes entirely and communicate in plain English. But even English isn't always the same. In New York City to "jack somebody up" means to beat them up; in Baltimore it means an aggressive frisk. Baltimore and New York City police have different terms for many similar items such as ambulance ("ambo" in Baltimore versus "bus" in New York), searching a suspect on the street ("jack-up" versus "toss"), beating a person ("thump" versus "jack-up"), an out-of-the-way place to rest ("hole" versus "coop"), and a good police officer ("real PO-lice" versus "cop's cop"). In her New York research, Elizabeth Reuss-Ianni discusses how police follow people who "look dirty"—that is, suspicious. In Baltimore, the word "dirty" is limited to an individual involved in drugs.

My language reflects the language of Baltimore City police officers: a suspect is never a perp but can be thirty-dash-one (from a box number 30-1 on an obsolete arrest report); an arrest is a lockup, never a collar; and a person's race is a number: blacks are number one and whites are number two. In 2000, Baltimore had very few number threes, any race other than white or black.

In general, any professional courtesy you receive as a police officer (not receiving a traffic ticket, free coffee, getting into a night club) decreases as distance increases, in part because of the inability to know with certainty that the person really is a police officer. In more casual social situations, police officers are not keen to identify themselves as police officers except when other police officers are around.

On a long weekend, I would often take the train or drive (alas, I could not ride Amtrak for free) to Brooklyn to visit my girlfriend. The quick transition from Baltimore ghetto to white Fort Greene hipster party could be quite abrupt. Admitting you're a police officer to a stranger at a party when she asks you what you do is always a gamble and usually a conversation stopper. The first response is inevitably, "Really?" Some then express admiration. Some want nothing to do with you. Some say they hate police officers. Some ask what it's like and want to hear stories. But most of these people are soft and blanch at real cop stories involving blood, suffering, and pain. Then I would have to excuse myself and get another beer.

In the end, class members saw the overall approach of the academy as ineffective: neither tough enough to serve as a boot camp, rigorous enough to impart knowledge, nor intelligent enough to encourage thinking. After three months in the academy, one trainee asked me, "Has a single week gone by where you can say that you learned *anything* every day? It's kind of sad, isn't it?" Another trainee said, "No wonder that's how cops are out there [rude to people]. They demean us. They break us down. But there is no buildup. It's like prison." Morale among police academy trainees was significantly lower by the end of the police academy.[13]

At the graduation ceremony, there is pomp, circumstance, and a handshake from the mayor. The first two months on the street are spent in "field training." More often than not, field trainers are motivated to work with the greenhorn trainees because of the extra money—an extra twelve dollars per shift in 2000. Armed with a badge, gun, and more questions than confidence, trainees go into the streets and learn how to be a cop.

CHAPTER 3

New Jack: Learning To Do Drugs

All right you maggots, let's lock people up! They
don't pay you to stand around. I want production! I
want lockups! Unlike the citizens of the Eastern
District, you are required to work for your
government check.

—*A Baltimore police sergeant motivating his squad
at shift change*

After the police academy, the first two months policing
are spent in "field training." Trainees in full uniform
and with the power of arrest patrol with more experienced
officers, "field training officers," in less desirable districts.
New police officers learn quickly. The full immersion of
police patrol in the ghetto is in marked contrast to the isolation of the police academy. Readily apparent are drug
addicts roaming the streets, drug dealers, families broken
apart, urban blight, rats, and trash-filled alleys. Inside
homes, things are often worse.

For most white and many black police officers, field
training is the first extended contact with the ghetto and
its residents. Police officers don't see the good. That's not
their job. Nobody calls 911 to report a graduation party, an
anniversary, or another hard day at work. People don't
need police when they're happy and everything is going
well. Police see misery at its best. Police are called into
people's homes because the residents have, at some level,
lost control: intensely overcrowded apartments next to
abandoned housing and empty lots, families without heat

or electricity, rooms lacking furniture filled with filth and dirty clothes, roaches and mice running rampant, jars and buckets of urine stacked in corners, and multiple children sleeping on bare and dirty mattresses. Simply entering a "normal" home, well furnished and clean, perhaps to take a stolen car report, is so rare that it would be mentioned to fellow officers.

Thug Life

While poverty is unquestionably rampant, many police (often using their own economically poor upbringing as evidence) are convinced the poverty does not create the ghetto. Rather, a ghetto culture of violence, sex, and drug use creates poverty. One officer told me, "You've seen what it's like. Can you imagine what it would be like if your professors knew what really goes on here? I don't see them walking down these alleys or spending time in one of these houses. They read about 280 murders, but they don't know about the thousand shootings, the cuttings, and assaults where people don't die. Those don't make the papers. If people saw how fucked up everything is, they'd stop blaming poverty or racism and just want the whole place torn down."

Most police, both white and black, believe that the social problems in the Eastern District are hopeless. One black officer said, "It's hard not to think that this is a jungle here. People running around in the street at all hours. Getting high, acting like fools . . . They ought to tear everything down. All of it!" A white officer echoed this belief: "I'd like to napalm the whole area. Wouldn't that be beautiful? Just come in with the air strikes and watch the whole thing go up in flames . . . I don't know what else you can do. If people want to live this way, I say fuck 'em."

A black officer proposed similar ends through different means. "If it were up to me," he said, "I'd build big walls and just flood the place. Biblical-like. Flood the place and start afresh. I think that's all you can do." When I asked this officer how his belief that the entire area be flooded differed from the attitudes of white police, he responded, "Naw, I'm not like that because I'd let the good people build an ark and float out. Old people, working people, line 'em up, two by two. White cops will be standing on the walls with big poles pushing people back in." The painful universal truth of this officer's beliefs came back to me in stark relief during the flooding and destruction of New Orleans, Louisiana. Police in some neighboring communities prevented displaced black residents from leaving the disaster area, turning them away with blockades and guns.

One officer compared policing the black ghetto to policing redneck white areas:

My philosophy is I hate everybody equally. We're dealing with shits no matter where we work. Everyone is going to lie to you. Those rednecks are just as bad [as blacks in the Eastern]. Same drinking, same domestics [violence], same kids, same welfare. But in Pigtown or South Baltimore [lower-class white neighborhoods] you'll see things you never get here, like incest and huffing [inhaling glue]. It's like one big Jerry Springer set. Pookie may not know who his daddy is, but half the time those [white] motherfuckers don't want to know! Plus they [whites] fight cops more. But it's strange because the same people who fight cops one day will help you out the next. Here [black] people just want nothing to do with you.

Another officer talked about Greektown, where I lived:

All those hillbillies. I'm surprised that they got Section 8 [public housing] there, with all the clout Greektown has. Those hillbillies come in and start selling drugs on the corner and bring their inbred cousins around. They've made the neighborhood a mess. It used to be good. And Fells Point has Mexicans moving in, but they're better than the hillbillies. At least the Mexicans want to work. They may be poor, but they don't trash their neighborhood and homes like the white trash does.

Police generally couch their hatreds in terms of class and culture, not race. When I half-jokingly accused my partner of just not liking black people, he responded passionately, "I got nothing against black people. I just don't like *these* black people. I don't care what color they are. If they were white people acting this way, I wouldn't like them any better. Hell, I'd probably like them worse."

The Addict

In the ghetto, police and the public have a general mutual desire to avoid interaction. The sociologist Ervin Goffman wrote, "One avoids a person of high status out of deference to him and avoids a person of lower status . . . out of a self-protective concern."[1] Goffman was concerned with the stigma of race, but in the ghetto, stigma revolves around the "pollution" associated with drugs. Police use words like filthy, rank, smelly, or nasty to describe literal filth, which abounds in the Eastern District. The word "dirty" is used to describe the figurative filth of a drug addict. It is, in the drug-related sense, the opposite of being clean. Addicts also refer to "getting cleaned up" as in, "I've been clean for one week." Still drug users and the police use the idea of dirty in slightly different ways. Addicts consider themselves dirty or clean depending on whether or not they have drugs on them. If stopped by police, addicts hustling to get money for drugs may protest that they are not dirty. Police refer to anybody who is or will be involved with drugs or anything drug-related as dirty.

The damage from hardcore addiction is self-evident, even to an only slightly trained eye. Many addicts have blemished and damaged skin, an awkward gait, missing teeth, a thin physique, and, while high on heroin, a gravity-defying ability to lean and sway without falling down. I often visited a local Laundromat owner who sits behind plexiglass and, for fear of robbery, opened at 7 AM and closed at 2 PM He described a heroin addict who did small odd jobs for him: "Frank was gone for thirteen months. Locked up. When he came back, things were different, but then [simulates repeated injection with his finger into his arm] He used to do good work. Plumbing, carpentry, electrical. He was making $18 an hour doing, what's it called? With brick. Laying bricks. And now he can't even clean windows." The owner kindly continued to offer Frank odd jobs until the addict burglarized the store for $300 in quarters. In the following days, the bar across the street was inundated with people using change for their liquor purchases.

"How could anyone start taking drugs here?" one police officer wondered. "All you got to do is look around to see how it fucks you up." Another officer and I were curious about the high the drug delivers. He said, "Can you imagine the high you get? People give up their family, their job, their home, and find themselves living in some vacant [building], pissing in a jar? Damn, that shit must be good!"

A white officer described his approach to drug addicts:

> Look, I treat everyone with respect. Even the junkies, I'll always start with "sir," "ma'am," or "Mr. Moskos." [A common police joke is to address a destitute, drunk, or crazy person by your partner's name.] . . . "Mr. Moskos, please get out of the gutter." You've got to treat everyone with respect. Most junkies will do whatever you say. They don't want a hassle. I'm not going to lock somebody up for one or two pills. But what they're doing is illegal. You see what drugs do to these people. If they don't respect themselves, I'm not going to respect them. But you never have to treat anybody like shit. Well, most of the time, anyway.

Similarly:

> How am I, as a Baltimore police officer, supposed to have empathy for a drug addict? How am I supposed to have empathy for a criminal?

Another officer builds on the theme of respect:

> How am I supposed to respect a junkie when he doesn't even respect himself? You want me to respect some crack ho? Say it's her choice to suck dicks for her next hit? Leave her kids sleeping in shit? Or some junkie injecting into his arm, burning down a vacant? I can't respect that. I pity it! But I don't respect that person.

A strong link connects dehumanizing or stigmatizing the addict and arresting junkies:

> Sarge really likes arrests, and I give them to him. . . . If I see a white junkie coming here to cop [buy drugs], I'll stop them. Conspiracy to possess. Loitering. I don't give a shit if they [state's attorney] won't take it. That's their problem. It's better than writing a rape or robbery report later. And it's just a junkie. Junkies don't have rights. They're not even people. Who gives a flying fuck about a junkie!?

It's easy to get frustrated at times. I was no exception. After five months on the street, I wrote in my notes:[2]

> Fucking junkie ass who pissed me off. At 5 AM we get a call for CDS [drugs] on 1800 E Lafayette. Upon arrival, there's a junkie guy wearing no pants (but he is wearing his boxers) who says he's having an asthma attack. I get out [and listen for wheezing, as I have asthma and am familiar with the signs] and don't hear shit. But he says he wants an ambulance. I tell him he doesn't need an ambo [ambulance]. I tell him to go home. He won't leave because he wants an ambo.
>
> We call for an ambulance and *then* he starts to walk away. I tell him to stay on the corner (now there's a switch) [since much of the police job is telling people to leave the corner]. He wants to cross the street, where he says his pants are (they're not there [my partner looked]). I grab his shirt and tell him to sit down and wait for the ambo. A woman across the street who says she's his sister starts yelling at me to let him go. I tell her an ambulance is coming. She says, "He don't need no ambo, just let him

go." I tell her to shut up. [A police officer would be held liable if such a person were allowed to leave and then became sick or died.]

Ambo comes. Of course he don't need no ambo. Guy leaves. Ambo [paramedics] upset because we woke them up. Now the guy will probably get beat down on North Ave or something. Others on the corner say he was talking about snakes on him (which is a common complaint [among people having a bad drug experience] and would explain the lack of pants). But what's up with this guy wanting an ambo while his junkie peoples saying he don't? Man, it gets tired, quick.

A retired white officer believed that black police officers are more likely to be compassionate to drug addicts: "If somebody in their family is addicted, a brother or father or son, so they're going to have a little more compassion for the addict. But white cops, you know how it is, it's 'junkie this' or 'junkie that.' They're not even considered people." Compassion toward addicts, however, is not universal among any race of police officers. One black police officer told me: "I got family who are junkies. I'd lock them up, too. You a junkie, off you go [to jail.]. . . . I don't respect them. How can I respect a junkie? I don't want my girl thinking taking drugs is OK. . . . Do I think jail is going to fix them? Well, *[laughs]* that depends on who their cellmate is. *[More seriously.]* Jail doesn't fix anybody. But junkies got to hit rock bottom before they want to get better. And me locking your ass up might make you want it just a little more."

Because of situation, poor life choices, and separation from working-class values, "junkies" are too often perceived as having willingly forfeited their natural, legal, and human rights. Police effectively dehumanize persons involved in the drug trade, labeling them drug dealers or junkies. Depending on political persuasion, outsiders tend to see drug dealers and drug addicts as criminals, victims, or entrepreneurs. Yet for those who live or work in ghettos, such distinctions matter little. The damage to the community from public dealers and addicts is real and severe. Neither, to put it mildly, makes a good neighbor.

Public Service?

Whether drugs are the cause or symptom of greater social problems is, from a police perspective, irrelevant: "If we could get rid of drugs, everything else would fall into place," said one officer. Another officer commented, "Anything we can do to make life harder for drug dealers and junkies helps." But minor disruptions of the drug trade can actually increase violence, and an obsession with drug addicts hurts the police. As police lose sympathy and empathy for the segment of the lower-class population most victimized by drug use and drug-related violence, the focus of police work shifts away from the academy ideal of helping and serving the public. Unchanged throughout the police academy, more than 60 percent of trainees—80 percent of black trainees and just under half of the white trainees—stated a desire to "help other people" as a major reason for becoming police.[3]After one year on the street, the percentage of officers claiming this motivation dropped by one-third, to 40 percent.[4]

On the street, as the trainee becomes a police officer, the desire to help or "serve" the public lessens as part of a greater shift from a public-centered ideal to more police-centered ideals: minimizing unpleasant dealings, avoiding paperwork, and getting home safely. An officer explained, "Sure, you start off wanting to do good, help people. But then you see how things are. All the junkies. Everybody lies. Victims won't tell you anything because they're criminals themselves. Then you start to ask, 'Why am I here?'" Another officer said, "People out here think it's normal to sell drugs. They've done it for generations. It pays the rent. And the rest use drugs. So why are they going to help us? Everybody here is dirty. They're all criminals. Even the ones who aren't criminals got family who are."

By having only limited contact with the noncriminal public, police officers perceive the criminal element as even larger than it is. A sergeant estimated, "Ninety-five percent of the people in Sector Two [of the Eastern District] are criminals or don't like the police. . . . The fact that people don't want the police or the court system are the two biggest problems." The normalcy of drug use was a frequent theme: "It's a different culture here. People don't think drugs are criminal. I mean, how many times have you heard people say, 'It's just for personal use.' We can't do our job. Half the people here are criminals. Another 30 percent don't care. . . . They don't care, so they get what they deserve." The same officer was more reflective later that night: "I wish I worked in an area where I cared. Where people thanked you for doing a good job. I did [care] the first few years. But then you just get tired. I'd like to work somewhere where people aren't always trying to get over on you. Shit, the people who are nice to you here are the ones you've got to watch out for, because they did something wrong. People [police officers] come from other districts and they have no clue. They can't tell who's bullshitting them and who's not because they're just not used to it. But you'll get a clue really fast."

Police officers also note the push of drug culture into the lives of those who aren't involved with drugs or the drug trade, per se. One officer commented, "Even those who don't sell drugs, they all sit around on the stoops trying to look like drug dealers. It's a fucked-up culture." Another said: "It's bad enough that you got all these punks out here, but the sad part is people actually *want* to be thugs. They idolize criminals. What the hell is 'thug life,' and why does all the rap music support it? Ray Lewis [a Baltimore Raven football player who beat double murder charges] symbolizes the city. A thug who should be in jail, but got away with it and is now voted [Superbowl] MVP."

A more liberal officer said: "All we can do is hold the tide. These people need parents. Maybe some religion. Something. Drugs is bad, but these people got issues that got nothing to do with drugs. People have to start investing in the city. In schools. Show the kids something better. But it'll take time."

Despite the ominous and threatening presence of a group of drug dealers sitting on a stoop, it is not illegal to *be* a drug dealer.[5] In practical terms, it is only *possession* of illegal drugs that lets police make a drug arrest. As drug dealers will usually delegate drug possession to an underling—and only the stupidest drug dealers sells drugs in the presence of a uniformed police officer or a marked patrol car—uniformed patrol officers are limited in the actions they may legally take against public drug dealers. Dealers are a constant and long-term presence. But a drug deal itself is quick—drugs can be ordered, bought, and received in a few seconds (more on this later).

In high-drug areas, there is no shortage of drug offenders to arrest. Though there are no statistics on the specific percentage of Eastern District residents using or addicted to drugs, drug usage rates are undoubtedly higher in the Eastern District than in the city overall, where the drug addiction rate is estimated to be 10 percent of the total population.[6] A large percentage of the population of the Eastern District, perhaps even an absolute majority, occasionally uses illegal drugs. One officer described the scene around an open-air drug market: "[This is an arrest] free-for-all. . . . *[Banging steering wheel of car]* Junkie, junkie, junkie! You can pull up to any corner and lock up everybody walking away [or] any white person you see. They're all dirty. . . . If you want court time, this is where you come. Fuckers come from other sectors, even the Southeast, just to poach from here [police come from other areas just to find arrests]. But there's plenty to go around. By the time we got the last, the first would be long out and we could start all over again." The decision to arrest or not arrest those involved in the drug trade becomes a matter of personal choice and police officer discretion more than any formalized police response toward crime or public safety.

Crimes and Misdemeanors

The formal rules of arrest learned in the police academy are seen as having limited practical application on the street. Learning to arrest involves three related but distinct facets: the informal standards for acceptable versus arrestable behavior, the formal legal standards of probable cause for arrest, and the informal rules within formal prosecution. A police officer has to know all the rules, when they apply, and how to follow them.

It takes very few appearances in court to see that the legal system is not a well-funded search for truth and justice. Courts are a game to be mastered by defendants, prosecutors, police officers, and judges alike. They all manipulate the system to serve their own interests.[7] On one hand, the overloaded system often fails to punish the guilty and dangerous. On the other hand, the system does little to accommodate crime victims or protect those falsely accused. The truly innocent, those who face charges without having a committed any crime, are very rare. But by being so rare, the presumption is almost always of guilt. The courts become a bottleneck on the road to prison. Police keep pouring the guilty into an already overflowing funnel. Baltimore's Circuit Court, for example, with a capacity to hold 500 jury trials a year, handles 10,000 felony cases annually.[8] In both the literal and figurative sense, justice is plea-bargained.

Informal rules on policing drugs are largely related to the requirements for effective prosecution in court. The formal constitutional rules—reasonable suspicion for a stop or frisk and probable cause for a search or arrest—are relatively easy to follow. The standards demanded by the local state's attorney for prosecution are much stricter and, as they can be unique to Baltimore City, are, to a certain degree, arbitrary. Police officers learn what prosecutors look for and demand in officers' charging documents and statements of probable cause. In the academy, an instructor had tried to make clear that "creative writing"—filling out reports and such—could be both clever and true. "There's a difference between 'creative writing' and lying," he said. "Don't get caught up in lying. Creative writing is utilizing what you have." He gave the example of an officer observing and articulating that a thrown bag of drugs was still warm to the touch on a winter day: "Otherwise the defense attorney could ask how the officer knew that it was his suspect who threw the bag, since the cop caught the suspect before going back to get the bag."

"The pen is mightier than the sword!" an older officer said in a bar one morning after work, "When I get done with this *[holding up his pen]*, you'll be amazed at the things you did." Even without resorting to perjury, officers have tremendous leeway and discretion in their report writing. Writing can indeed be creative, but on the street the term "creative writing" is generally synonymous with lying and perjury, a crime that jeopardizes career and pension. Informal rules state first and foremost to "cover your ass." Lying on a charging document "leaves your ass hanging in the wind to anybody with a video camera." The threat of job termination is seen to outweigh the benefits of convicting the guilty.

On my fifth day out of the academy, my field trainer and I responded to a street corner for a larceny. We were met by an elderly man and his son. It was hard to get information from the man, who was a bit senile. He had a hunch that a known female acquaintance had taken a gun from his house. He did not, however, witness the event nor have any proof. The man wanted us to go to the woman's address, confront the woman, and return his gun. We refused his request and advised the man that citizens could seek warrants from the court commissioner. The man's son did not know if his father had simply lost the gun but insisted the gun was legal, even though there was no proof of ownership.

In the original report, I had softened the statements and tone of the man, but retained the "facts" as related by the "victim":

> On 10 April 2000 at 1235 hours, we responded to Harford and North Ave. for a larceny. Upon arrival, Mr. Boyd stated that he believes someone may have stolen his gun. The gun was last seen approximately one month ago and was kept on a shelf in a closet at 1687 E Preston St Apt. #214.
>
> Investigation revealed that Mr. Boyd believes that Ms. Mildred "Squeaky" (unknown last name) of 2170 N Port St., who has access to the apartment, may have taken the gun. However he is not sure. Mr. Boyd is an elderly gentleman and stated that his memory is poor. Mr. Boyd does not recall if he moved the gun.

My field training officer did not accept this report. This was a case of lost property, and theft has no place in a lost property report. The rewrite, true in words if not spirit, stated:

> On 10 April 2000 at 1235 hours, we responded to Harford and North Ave. Upon arrival, we met Mr. Boyd. Mr. Boyd is an elderly gentleman who stated that his memory is poor. Mr. Boyd does not know what happened to his gun. The gun was last seen approximately one month ago and was kept on a shelf in his closet at 1687 E. Preston St. Apt. #214. Mr. Boyd does not recall moving the gun nor does he know its whereabouts.

Had the first version of the report been submitted, it would have counted as a Part One larceny in the FBI's Uniform Crime Report. Even if the gun were legal and had been stolen, based on what we had, we could do very little to retrieve it. In the final version, no crime occurred and no further police investigation was required. In hindsight and with more experience, I probably would have investigated one step further and seen if "Squeaky" could be found, even knowing full well that "Squeaky" would not admit to anything even on the chance she was guilty.

The reason this report was rewritten had everything to do with avoiding messy paperwork and very little to do with lowering the reported crime rate. In my time in Baltimore, I never felt any pressure to suppress or misinterpret crime statistics. One night at roll call, there was talk about Internal Affairs being on the lookout for false reports, the commanding officer said, "If somebody says something to you, write it down as they say. Don't try to save us crime. Save your job first. . . . It doesn't matter if it doesn't sound 'right.'" But it would be very easy to finagle crime statistics, especially in the gray areas of assault—common versus aggravated—and lent, lost, or stolen property.

One night I received a call for a domestic assault at 905 Chapel, but there are no buildings on the 900 block of Chapel St. A colleague gleefully told me he tracked down the woman at 905 Castle St. and, since it wasn't his call, added with delight, "She's a real stinker!" The woman, in her fifties, looked much older. She was so drunk I could barely understand her. But I did hear her say that a friend pushed her down the stairs and she's sick of it. There were no signs of minor injury, much less a fall down the stairs.

I could smell from the sidewalk that she and the house stank to high heaven. When I tried to get the woman's information, two officers entered the house but didn't get far. They gagged and made a quick exit.

"Why's it so stinky?" I asked the woman.
"He don't bathe. Not in a year."
"Why not?"
"He lazy."
"That's pretty lazy," I said, "because once you get in the tub, bathing kind of takes care of itself."

I wondered if she made the whole thing up. Or if she wasn't pushed but fell. After all, she couldn't stand without leaning on something for support. I wondered if there even was a man inside. Even if there were, he would just say he didn't do anything. There wasn't much I could do because she had no signs of injury. At least that's how I rationalized it. Mostly I didn't want to go in the house and puke. I changed the call from domestic assault to domestic dispute. She certainly wouldn't remember anything in the morning.

The officer who found the woman laughed,
"Dispute?! 'I was assaulted! He pushed me down the stairs!'"
I told him I didn't hear that.
"Oh, look at the slippery slope . . . writing false reports. That's the beginning!"
"So where do you draw the line?" I asked him.
"*[Jokingly]* I.I.D. [internal affairs] or jail. No, *[seriously]* when it's criminal. That's a clear line to me. And you?"
I had to think for a while. "I'll draw the line if someone goes to jail."

"You wouldn't arrest someone for loitering even if they weren't?"

"No. I haven't. I might violate the spirit of the [loitering] law, but not the letter of the law."

Another night, the same officer and I were driving down a street. A poorly dressed thirty-year-old white woman with heroin-related skin blemishes was walking toward a drug corner. My partner asked me to stop, got out of the car, and said to her: "You're here copping again. *What* did I tell you last time I saw you?" He quickly arrested the woman. He charged the woman with loitering and wrote on his report that the woman had been issued a warning prior to arrest, one requirement of Baltimore's loitering law. I questioned him, "I didn't see you issue any warning to that woman." He told me the details not in the report: "I did warn her. Last week. I told her if I saw her here again I would lock her up for loitering." So he did.

Although it is legally questionable, police officers almost always have something they can use to lock up somebody, "just because." New York City police use "disorderly conduct." In Baltimore it is loitering. In high-drug areas, minor arrests are very common, but rarely prosecuted. Loitering arrests usually do not articulate the legal required "obstruction of passage." But the point of loitering arrests is not to convict people of the misdemeanor. By any definition, loitering is abated by arrest. These lockups are used by police to assert authority or get criminals off the street.

A field training officer and I received a call for two people using drugs on a bench on Monument Street, a busy business district. We found a white couple sitting on the bench and a one dollar bill next to one of them. The training officer picked up the dollar bill and found a small amount of powder cocaine on it. The officer said, "We got a call for people using drugs on this bench and this bill was right by your hands." The officer searched them and found no other drugs. The couple complained about police not having the right to search them. The police officer looked at them quizzically, saying, "I've just told you my probable cause. We get this call for drugs and this bill is right next to you." My partner shook the cocaine from the bill and put it on the ground. He turned back to the two: "It's not yours, right?"

"No, it's not mine."

"You see," my partner said, "if it's nobody's bill, we'd have to submit it to lost property. . . . All right, whose dollar bill is this?" After three calls, a guy some distance away said, "It's my dollar!" and came and took it. We gave the happy stranger the dollar bill and let the white couple walk south toward Butchers Hill.

I asked my partner why he didn't simply arrest the couple for drug possession. The probable cause for arrest was indeed solid, based on the idea of constructive possession—like the papers on your desk or the gun in your car's glove compartment, the drugs at your feet belong to you if you know they're there and can pick them up. My field trainer schooled me in the legal realities: "Did you see them put the bill on the bench?" I hadn't. Neither had he. He continued: "Then you can't prove it's theirs, unless you want to start perjuring yourself. You've got three choices. The state's attorney won't press charges on constructive possession. If you don't follow the drugs from their hands to your pocket, you can forget about it. [So] we can lock them up for possession, do the paperwork, submit the drugs, and have them walk; [or] you can take an hour [and] submit the bill with the drugs as lost property; or we can pretend we never saw the drugs and give the lost dollar to its rightful owner." A black officer on foot watched the whole scene from nearby and shook her head. She muttered to me, "I don't like these shenanigans. I don't do [police work on] drugs. . . . I do my job and go home."

With a different field training officer, I received a call from a lady who said an addict accused her of taking his money, and then slapped her and spit on her. He lived down the block so we banged on his door, which swung wide open. A groggy man lying on his couch got up and a pill of heroin fell off him. He protested, "It's for personal use . . . I wasn't doing nothing." Though both statements were technically true, we arrested the man as the law demands. In the station, another officer made fun of this small-scale bust by calling my training officer "the one-hit wonder." The officer defensively pleaded, "I've got a trainee. We have to do that [arrest drug offenders 'by the book']." But, as I later learned, the more common informal rules for such a situation would be to ignore or destroy the pill, a "don't seek, don't flaunt" rule akin to "don't ask, don't tell."

At 7:30 AM, a few minutes before the entire shift would be called in for shift change, an officer stood on the sidewalk with a forlorn fifty-year-old African American man. The addict had his pockets inside-out and his few belongings—an almost empty pack of Newport menthol cigarettes, a lighter, loose change, keys, many scraps of paper, a metal bottle cap, a hypodermic needle, and one pill of heroin—piled on the sidewalk. The officer, wanting to go home, skeptically asked the others at the scene, "Anybody want a lockup? Good overtime?" I and everybody present declined, one squadmate went so far as to point at the officer while laughing, "*Ha*-ha!" imitating Nelson Muntz from *The Simpsons*. With no takers, the searching officer kicked the needle and pill into the gutter and crushed them with his boots. The addict visibly winced as they were destroyed. The officer removed his latex gloves, dropped them in the gutter, and returned the addict's jail-issued state ID card. "You're getting a break," he told the addict. "Go home." The addict picked up his remaining belongings and said, "Yes, sir. Thank you, sir. You won't see me again," and quickly limped away.

On my first night on patrol after field training, two other officers and I were out of our cars when two drug dealers walked toward us. One of the officers told me, "Watch his hands." As the two suspects were being questioned by the other officers, I went and looked on the sidewalk where the two suspects had come from. I found a vial with cocaine. I brought the vial back, thinking this would help the cause. One officer asked me if I had seen the suspects drop the vial. I told him I hadn't. He rolled his eyes and told me, "If you don't see him drop it, just kick it or crush it. Now you've got to write a found property [report] in case someone saw you pick it up. Because if you dump it now, it could come back to bite you." It took forty-five minutes, time I could have been patrolling, to submit this ten-dollar vial of crack for destruction.

To meet the standards needed for a formal prosecution, one must follow the informal rules imposed by the state's attorney. Rule number one is don't take your eyes off the drugs. Drug charges against a suspect will not be prosecuted in Baltimore City if an officer fails to maintain constant sight of the drugs. A suspect fleeing from police will throw down drugs while running. An officer in foot pursuit must then choose between catching a suspect with no drugs or retrieving the drugs with no suspect. Officers generally will choose to follow the suspect over the drugs because— along with a personal desire to catch a fleeing suspect—arrests are a police statistic used to judge performance. Found drugs are not.

After catching the suspect, the officer will return to retrieve the drugs and charge the suspect with possession, knowing full well that the charges will be dropped if the report is written honestly. But officers are rewarded for arrests, not convictions. If the drugs can't be found—lost in weeds, scooped up by a bystander, or never there to begin with—the officer is in a bit of a bind, left with the noncrime of "felony running." You can't lock somebody up for drug possession without drugs. And after a chase, even loitering doesn't apply. But the officer will find some crime, however minor. If you run and get caught, you're probably not sleeping in your own bed that night.

If one views drug addiction as a medical problem rather than a criminal concern, then one should question the benefit of locking up addicts. Some claim, perhaps well intentioned but ultimately incorrectly, that informal police discretion equals corruption. The officer's actions in destroying drugs and inaction in failing to arrest a man guilty of drug possession are punishable at the departmental and perhaps even criminal level. But destroying the drugs makes moral and fiscal sense. The addict needs help the criminal justice system can't and won't give him. Proper drug submission would cost the city needless overtime pay and increased the opportunity for corruption as the drugs work their way toward, one hopes, eventual destruction. Each arrest costs the city hundreds and sometimes thousands of dollars. The shame, at least from the police officers' perspective, is that in exercising wise discretion and doing the right thing, they violate their oath to uphold the laws of the land. It is unfortunate and ironic that such heady decisions come not from noble ideals and open debate, but from the stronger and more universal motivation to go home after a long night's work.

My Fair Lady: A Note on Street Slang

Police need to learn the language and dialect of the people they police. In East Baltimore, most residents speak African American Vernacular English. East Baltimore combines a ghetto style of speech with pronunciation unique to Baltimore. Cars have "tags." "Baby's father" and "baby's mother" are the most common terms for one's child's mother or father. To "fall out" is to faint while "left out" is the past tense of leave. "Zinc" is sink. "Bank" means to hit. "Bounce" is to leave. "Chillin'" is not causing trouble. "Boo" is an affectionate and diminutive term. "Hoppers" are young trouble makers typically wearing "the uniform" of white T-shirts, baggie jeans, and Timberlands shoes. The youngest of the "hoppers" may be called a "bopper." A "yo-boy" starts his sentences with "yo." "Peoples" describes friends while a "cousin" is a close friend. "Selling woof tickets" is to talk "junk." "Police" is always stressed on the first syllable—"PO-lice." Pen is "ink pin." Dog is pronounced "dug." Heroin is "Hair-ron." Hopkins hospital is "Hot-kins." You say the "Ham" in Durham Street but not the "T" in Baltimore. And, it being Baltimore, you can always say "Hon" with a straight face.

Language extends to a couple's sexual history. While personally none of my business, knowing if two people had ever had sex was part of my job. All calls must be categorized as "domestic" or "non-domestic related." The legal rules change for disputes involving people who have had sex, the Maryland definition of "domestic." Only in "domestics" can police arrest for a misdemeanor they did not witness. Only in "domestics" are police virtually required to arrest for all assaults, no matter how minor. Only in "domestics" can police arrest somebody as a preventive measure if the other party is afraid (and has good reason to be afraid). Only in "domestics" do police have to write a report for every incident, bar none. The best question to ask is, "What is he [or she] to you?" But that requires the person to know what I'm really getting at. If the answer is, "a friend," one had to be more direct. "Fuck" gets to the point but is too crude. "Have you ever had sex?" sounds like you're blaming the victim. "Have you two ever been romantically involved?" would get laughs and implies a level of romance that may be inappropriate. "What kind of relationship do you have?" borders on psychotherapy. Slang words abound, but "tapping it," "touching it," or "spanking it" ("it," of course, being "that ass"), are too informal and somewhat gender specific. To tactfully and efficiently learn a couple's sexual history is a minor art. The best phrase I used was, "Have you two ever hit it?" Linguistically "hitting it" allowed all parties to maintain some decorum and allows a simple yes or no answer.

As both a source of amusement and a more effective form of communication, police adapt local lingo. Police officers' spouses frequently complain when ghetto language is brought home from work. One officer said, "My old lady gets pissed off whenever we have an argument because I start speaking ghettoese. 'Why you gotta sound like a yo?'" A field trainer warned me, "You can't help it. After a while you start to talk like them."

Arguably nothing may sound more racist than a bunch of white cops imitating, not always accurately, black ghetto speech. But standard American English can be a barrier to communication and effective policing. One time a boy, approximately five-years-old, told me he couldn't understand me because I spoke fast, "like those men on TV." Another time I knocked on the door of a house and loudly announced myself using my natural Midwest-born style of speech: "p'-LEES." A young girl on the other side said, "Who?" I repeated myself twice but was not understood. Finally I affected a Baltimore accent and said, "PO-lice" in the Southern way. I heard the girl run to her mom and say, using local slang for police, "Ma, the po-po's at the do' [door]!"

A white officer said, "When I first came on the job, I couldn't understand 90 percent of what these motherfuckers were saying. But then I learned ghettoese. You know, like Chinese, Japanese. This is ghettoese." An African American cop told me he was trilingual: "I'm from here. I speak three languages: English, bad English, and profanity!" Fresh on the street, I explained to one of my white academy classmates that the word "cousin" was not to be taken literally. He later thanked me and explained to another squadmate: "When I first came on I would get pissed off when people would call someone [a nonrelative] their cousin. I thought they were lying to me and I would get offended. But then Moskos explained to me that that's just the way they talk. So now I ask them if someone is a real cousin, or just a cousin cousin."

At times, I would occasionally break tension with a judicious use of "true 'dat." The meaning is obvious: simple agreement. But since white people do not really use the expression, the phrase would cause a double take and a brief smile or laugh. Early one morning I saw a man on a bicycle talking very loudly to a woman. I went closer to make sure everything was OK.

> They're both smiling and I hear the woman saying, "I'm gonna miss you!"
>
> I pulled up to the man and said hopefully, "she's gonna miss you."
>
> He turned to me and rolled his eyes: "I get off work at 2:30 and make tips. It's five o'clock now and she's got my money and says she's going to miss me. She ain't gonna miss me one bit. If she was, she wouldn't be leaving!"
>
> "True 'dat."
>
> "What?"
>
> "True 'dat. She ain't gonna miss you."
>
> *[Laughing]* "Look at that, the PO-lice saying 'true 'dat.' All right, you be safe man."

CHAPTER 4

The Corner: Life on the Streets

> It's a different culture. You know, what is normal for
> us—like going to work, getting married—they don't
> understand that. Drugs are normal. Mommy did it.
> Daddy did it, not that he's around. But if people
> want to take drugs, there's nothing we can do. All
> we can do is lock them up. But even that is normal.
>
> —*A Baltimore City police officer*

The drug-dealing block is a buzz of constant activity. Dealers hawk their wares, customers come and go, and addicts roam the street hustling for their next hit. Occasionally a police car will appear and the street crowd will disperse, slowly walking away from the police car. Being too fast or too slow can make oneself a conspicuous mark for police attention. So people walk, shuffle, and roll with a well practiced nonchalance. Soon after the appearance of a police car, the street will be deserted. When the police car leaves, the crowd returns.

The Eastern District's 45,000 residents account for over 20,000 arrests every year.[1] Most arrests are drug related.[2] Police officers patrol in their cars, respond to 911 calls, and clear corners. These officers, who by and large hate the ghetto, are frustrated to see those arrested go free in the revolving door of the criminal justice system: "justice for criminals," goes the well worn police cliché. The cycle repeats. Police earn court overtime pay while residents get rap sheets. It's a horrible equilibrium, and police are the fulcrum.

The Baltimore Police Department estimates that 80 percent of homicides are drug related. Most of these murders are not big news. A twelve person shooting at an "RIP party" for a drug dealer who had himself been murdered was not even page-one news in the *Baltimore Sun*. The violence of Baltimore's drug trade may be extreme, but it is typical of drug-related violence: poor young men, usually black, with access to guns, involved in illegal public drug dealing.[3]

Police rarely witness the actual drug deal. Police see the signs and the aftermath of what occurs on the street, but in many ways know very little. After a year on the street, 94 percent of patrol officers believe that citizens know more about what goes on in an area than the officers who patrol there.[4] Police response to an active drug corner follows a standard modus operandi: a citizen calls 911, a responding police car approaches, drug activity stops, and people—dealers, friends, addicts, lookouts, and any "innocents" who happen to be walking by—will slowly walk away.

Most often, the suspects will go for a brief walk around the block and then, after police leave, reconvene on the same or a nearby stoop. Dispersing without being asked is considered a sign of criminal activity, or perhaps an outstanding warrant. But police also view quick and unprompted departure—walking, not running—as a sign of respect and a satisfactory resolution to most problems. On one such call, I pulled up to a stoop and two drug suspects walked without being asked. My partner happily said, "I love respectful drug dealers." We drove away.

Clearing the corner is what separates those who have policed from those who haven't. Some officers want to be feared. Others simply respected. An officer explained: "You don't have to [hit anybody]. Show up to them. Tell them to leave the corner, and then take a walk. Come back, and if they're still there, don't ask questions, just call for additional units and a wagon. You can always lock them up for something. You just have to know your laws. There's loitering, obstruction of a sidewalk, loitering in front of the liquor store, disruptive behavior." Police assume that if the suspects are dirty, they will walk away rather than risk being stopped and frisked. You *can* always lock them up for something, but when a police officers pulls-up on a known drug corner, legal options are limited.

Clocking in and Clocking out

Street-level drug operations are called "shops" because of their operators' business-centered outlook. But most are not professional operations. One elderly resident complained, "I've been here fifty-six years and it's just gotten worse and worse. I don't sit on the stoop like I used to. Those drug dealers just have no respect. Not for the elderly. Not for kids. For nothing!" Corner drug dealing has five distinct jobs or positions: lookouts, steerers, money-man, slinger, and gunman. In practice, these roles can be amorphous. More often than not, one person handles multiple positions, but a cardinal rule of drug dealing is to keep the money and the drugs separate. A careful dealer will always separate himself from those who handle drugs or money, limiting everyone's legal liability. There are other positions in a drug operation—the couriers or runners who transport drugs, the cookers who cook crack, the packers who package drugs in $10 or $20 units for resale—that are not actively present in the street-level drug trade and therefore not the focus of a post officer.

A young addict once approached me in my patrol car. He said he wanted to be my confidential informant so I could "take out" a drug house. When pressed, he admitted that he was pissed off at the people in the drug house. He worked as a lookout for them, but one time, "the police were right up on me so I didn't call them out." As punishment, he was beaten so bad that he needed stitches in his head.

This was two weeks before my last night at work, so I had no interest. There was little point in me making arrests when I wouldn't be around for court, but our conversation continued. I asked him how much heroin he took. He said it depended on how much money he had. This day he was flush so he bought seven pills ($70). But he quickly added, "I don't always have the money." He had just turned twenty-two and had been shooting up heroin for nine months. His skin still looked good. Interestingly he wondered why you can get high from snorting and shooting heroin but not from swallowing. "That just makes me sick. But I don't get it. It gets in your bloodstream either way." I didn't have the answer.

I asked him how much he made working the corner and he gave me income figures for various jobs. Working as a uniformed police officer, income data gathered from drug addicts is questionable at best, but his figures are supported by academic studies and police officers familiar with the drug trade.[5]

Lookouts are the lowest job in the drug operation. Almost always an addict, a lookout has the simple job of alerting others when police are approaching. Any holler will do, such as the common "five-oh," slang for police from the TV show "Hawaii Five-O," or "whoop whoop," the sound of a quickly toggled police siren. A lookout will make about thirty-five to fifty dollars a day and is often paid in drugs. While the quality of lookouts is often poor, it's not a tough job. Pay is bad because there is no shortage of citizens in East Baltimore willing to "call out" cops gratis.

The steerer, hawker, or tout is responsible for promoting the product and leading the customer to the seller. A steerer can hail those driving by with a wave or a well-known sign to hail an unlicensed taxi—a "hack." Hacks are an illegal but common practice in Baltimore and are hailed by holding an arm out and flapping the hand down and up, usually with the fingers together. For local customers, a steerer may walk down the street shouting a brand name that represents a certain batch of drugs. Vials are usually marketed according to the color of the plastic stopper top, as in "Red Tops" or "Black Tops." Crack is often sold under the generic name "ready-rock." Cocaine, both crack and powder, is sold in small plastic-topped glass vials legally used for holding essential oils and perfumes. Heroin in Baltimore is sold in gel capsules under slightly more creative names such as "Uptown," "Body Bag," or "Capone."

Customarily new "brands" are introduced at the beginning of the month to coincide with the arrival of welfare, social security, and disability checks. Drug markets boom when many are comparatively flush with cash. Before checks arrive, when money is scarce, dealers will promote the strength and purity of their new "brands" with free "testers." Good promotions at the end of the month can help sales the next week. Overdoses, ironically, are good for business.[6] A local resident described the phenomenon: "I seen it so many times. . . . Just this corner. [In the five years] I've been here, I've seen thirteen or fourteen people overdose. Just right around here. People come in and say, 'So-and-so OD'd!' And the drug dealers just laugh. They say, 'See, that's good shit.'"

While the jobs of both lookout and steerer are often freelanced to local addicts, the moneyman or "bank" holds the money and is therefore a position of some responsibility. A customer arranges the type, price, and quantity of a drug sale with the moneyman (who is not always a man). Most street-level transactions are for ten or twenty dollars. A good banker takes the money and holds no drugs. Holding money is not a crime, but when a person is arrested with money and drugs, the money may be seized under civil forfeiture laws. It is very hard to legally seize money from a person without drugs.

The slinger—slinging is also a term used for drug dealing in general—looks after and distributes the drugs. Because the criminal justice system treats juveniles more leniently, many slingers are under eighteen. After money is paid, the slinger gives the drugs to the buyer, a process known as "hitting off." Standard operating procedure is to access a hidden stash of drugs as needed. The stash, containing perhaps a few dozen pills of heroin and vials of cocaine, is kept nearby in weeds, trash, alleys, holes in lampposts, windowsills, or abandoned buildings. Slingers can make up to $200 a day but face the greatest risk of arrest. A boss does not typically cover bail or other arrest-related expenses for his crew.

Unless a suspect is caught with a large amount of drugs, Baltimore public prosecutors working for the Office of the

State's Attorney will not press charges for drug dealing. "Intent to distribute" (dealing) is automatically reduced to "possession" (personal use) for any amount less than twenty-five pieces of heroin and cocaine. At first I did not believe that city prosecutors would *automatically* reduce intent charges to possession based on amount rather than circumstance. Such a claim seems too much like police urban myth. I was convinced when I saw a piece of paper taped to the wall in the court liaison's office at Central Booking spelling out the policy. Slingers should and usually do hold fewer units of drugs than the amount required to be prosecuted "with intent" in Baltimore City.

The fifth and final position in any successful shop is the gunman responsible for protection. Because drug dealers are unable to turn to the police for protection, they regularly experience stickups and robberies.[7] The risk of a police frisk or search means that gunmen will usually not carry a weapon on their person, but rather keep the gun nearby, easily accessible.

Dealers tend to "open shop" during the 8 AM police shift-change and operate through the day and evening.[8] A limited number of drug corners operate twenty-four hours a day, seven days a week. While bad weather slows the drug trade, drug dealers display a hardy work ethic in even the worst weather. Some dealers operate locally, but a common tactic is to come from a different neighborhood and rent out a place, offering payment in drugs or money. Other dealers will simply squat a vacant building as a "stash house" and begin selling. Drug dealing occurs on public streets because of the ease and speed with which dealers may close shop when a lookout calls-out the police. The "foot soldiers," the workers, simply walk away. Drugs, and only a small amount, should be limited to just one crew member, the slinger. Mobility is a big asset. Dealing from a home presents greater risks. One police raid can ruin it all. The drug squad in particular is notoriously harsh in its tactics during home raids.

Street-level busts have little impact on the overall drug trade. On only one occasion was I aware of a period of even a few hours when drug addicts were unable to buy drugs because nobody was selling. Near the corner of Wolfe and Eager, my squad arrested a few drug dealers overnight. The FBI conducted a drug raid the following morning a few doors down. These arrests and the combined (though completely coincidental) federal and local presence closed the corner for a few hours. Addicts were audibly worried about being unable to buy their morning fix. The sugar supply by the corner laundromat's coffee pot was hit hard as massive quantities of sugar were downed to take some of the edge off the early stages of withdrawal. After shift change, judging from calls coming for the next shift, the corner was selling again, back in full swing and off the hook.

If a shop is run efficiently, the boss, himself working for or with a midlevel dealer, should be able to sit and observe the operation. By not handling drugs or money, he faces little risk of arrest from uniformed patrol officers. The boss may be sitting on a stoop of a nearby vacant and boarded-up building posted with a "no loitering" sign. Because of the sign, he could be arrested for the very minor charge of loitering, the catch all arrest charge. But how often can that be done? Repeated arrests for loitering, especially if no drugs are found, could easily result in a complaint about police racism and harassment to Internal Affairs.

Addicts make easy and docile arrest targets, but the arrest of one addict does nothing to close a drug market. Nor is it illegal for a lookout to call the police out by yelling "hootie-hoo" in a singsong voice every time a police car comes into sight. A moneyman can legally hold any amount of cash. Conspiracy to distribute drugs is a possible criminal charge, but impossible to prove without a long-term investigation, a route not open to patrol officers. The only person of the drug crew in obvious and convictable violation of the law is the slinger possessing and handing off drugs to the buyer.

If police are lucky, they may find the drug stash left behind by the dispersing group. If police find a supply of drugs and don't make an arrest—in police parlance: ripping a stash without a body—they would seize the contraband as "found property." While a seizure without an arrest entails paperwork and does not help an officer's "stats," police know that for a dealer, the long-term implications of losing a $1,000 stash are more severe than a few hours in jail and a future court date. Replacing $1,000 isn't easy. In the drug game, pay is less than many people believe.

It's the so-called tournament model of finance: if one is able to survive and rise up in the organizational hierarchy, there is the potential to make a lot of money. But most people working the corner make less than they would at McDonald's. Many Chicago gang members, as documented in an excellent study of gang finances, also held legal jobs.[9] But even McDonald's doesn't want to hire barely literate convicted felons with gold teeth and attitudes. People deal drugs in part because the legal job market offers few real alternatives. Pay in the street-corner drug trade can average out to less than minimum wage, but a little spending cash is better than none at all.[10]

Even with low pay, street corner drug dealing isn't all bad. The job has no commute, no piss test, you can work outside with friends, and drink on the job. And the work itself, as they say, isn't rocket science. "People wanna get high," says comedian Chris Rock, "Drugs sell themselves. It's crack. It's not an encyclopedia. It's not a fucking vacuum cleaner. You don't really gotta *try* to sell crack. I never heard a crack dealer go, 'Man, how am I gonna get rid of all this crack!?' "[11] If one is on the block anyway, why not clock-in and get paid? And the job has some perks: there are psychological pleasures in criminal behavior;[12] gangsta rap glamorizes the lifestyle; and there's a matter of respect. Drug dealers get laid.

Still the risk of death is astoundingly high. For some of those "in the game," the risk of death may be as high as 7 percent annually.[13] Each year in Baltimore's Eastern District approximately one in every 160 men aged fifteen to thirty-four is murdered. At this rate, *more than 10 percent of men in Baltimore's Eastern District are murdered* before the age of thirty-five.[14] As shocking as this is, the percentage would be drastically higher if it excluded those who aren't "in the game" and at risk because of their association with the drug trade. Yet if everybody you know has been shot, killed, or locked-up, perhaps such is life. In all my *juvenile* arrests (and I would assume adults as well, but officers are only responsible for checking priors on juveniles), I never locked anybody up for the first time. Even my youngest prisoners, two four-feet-tall thirteen-year-olds arrested for armed robbery on Christmas Eve, had rap sheets for drug dealing and attempted rape going back to when they were eleven. In the ghetto there is often little knowledge or appreciation of life and opportunities outside the ghetto.[15] That's why it's called the ghetto.

The largest causes of drug murders are territorial disputes over market share.[16] If no one will help you defend your property—you can't trademark the winning name that you've given your drugs, you can't take a competing drug dealer to court when he tries to take over your corner, you can't sue for libel if someone says your product is defective, it's not even in your interest to call the police if someone *shoots you*—then you have to protect yourself with your own hands. And the easiest way is with a gun. In a New York study, one-third of homicide victims were identified by police as "low-level" sellers, people involved in drug buying and selling mainly to support a personal habit. Only 4 percent of suspects and victims of violence were identified as kingpins who buy and sell drugs as a business primarily to make a profit.[17]

In one study from postarrest interviews, one-third to one-half of all juvenile drug sellers admitted to regularly carrying a gun.[18] Twenty percent of arrested juveniles and 31 percent of arrested admitted gang members claimed to carry guns all or most of the time.[19] Nine percent of those arrested agree with the statement, "It is OK to shoot someone who disrespected you."[20] This figure rises to 21 and 34 percent for drug sellers and gang members, respectively. But no association was found between drug *users* and guns. Some of the boasting about "being strapped" must be discounted as bravado. Police don't find many guns when frisking suspects. The threat of arrest may outweigh the risk of being robbed or attacked.[21] For others, a reputation for violence may be enough of a deterrent. Yet there is no doubt that guns are accessible to many. After all, gunfire is a daily reality and pacifist corner drug dealers don't last long.

Who's Your Dealer?

Baltimore's Eastern District is almost exclusively African American. The vast majority of drug buyers are local. However, white people from outlying areas form an extremely conspicuous consumer minority. People come to buy drugs because drugs in East Baltimore are better, both purer and cheaper than elsewhere. The archetypal white addict is employed, comes with a friend, drives a beat-up car from a nearby blue-collar neighborhood or suburb such as Highlandtown or Dundalk, and may have a local black drug addict in the back seat of the car. A black police officer who grew up in the Eastern District explained the local's presence, "White people won't buy drugs alone because they're afraid to get out of the car and approach a drug dealer. They'll have some black junkie with them." The local resident serves as a sort of freelance guide, providing insurance against getting "burned" or robbed. The local addict is paid informally, most often taking a cut of the drugs purchased. Occasionally—as evident from the surprising number of white people who call 911 and report that they were robbed of twenty dollars—the local does not return at all.

In cities like Chicago and Los Angeles, gangs control the drug dealing.[22] Because of that, some assume that drug violence is intrinsically linked to gangs. But East Coast cities have a different history. Large-scale gangs, such as the Bloods and Crips, are growing but still comparatively small. Gangs in Baltimore tend to be smaller and less organized, sometimes just a group sitting on a corner. Any group selling drugs can be called a gang, but the distinction between a gang and a group of friends is often based more on race, class, and police labeling than anything else.[23] The disorganization of Baltimore's crime networks may contribute to Baltimore's violence.[24] Conceivably organized large gangs could reduce violence by deterring competition and would-be stick-up kids.

While drug-dealing organizations exist, they tend to restrict themselves to wholesale operations without conspicuous gang names, clothes, or colors. In Baltimore, wholesalers—often SUV-driving Dominicans and Jamaicans with New York or Pennsylvania tags—will sell their product to various midlevel dealers once or twice a week. The midlevel dealers will "re-up" the corner dealers' "stash" as needed. Street-level dealers in Baltimore control smaller areas, perhaps three or four corners in close proximity. As a uniformed patrol officer, my focus was exclusively on the low-level street dealer. Going up the drug ladder requires lengthy investigations, undercover police, snitches, and confidential informants. A patrol officer's job is to answer 911 calls for service.

In America, most illegal drugs are sold peacefully and privately among middle-class suburbanites. Violence stems from the minority of drug deals that happens in urban public locales. As exemplified in Baltimore's Eastern District, these dealings are defined by three basic traits: outdoor selling, profits based on high volume, and violence.[25] Groups of young people, mostly but not exclusively men, sit on stoops or stand on street corners and conduct a brisk trade buying and selling heroin, cocaine, and marijuana. Just as most drug users occasionally sell drugs, most drug sellers regularly use drugs.[26] Many users become small-time sellers during brief periods of economic need. While an individual *can* sell drugs solo on the street, the risk of criminal robbery and police arrest tend to deter these individuals from selling over a long period of time. Drugs sold by small-time or temporary dealers are more likely to be "cut" (adulterated) or "burn" (fake). Substances similar in appearance to cocaine, such as baking soda, corn starch, or drywall, can be passed off as authentic. For users, the impurities in drugs are often more dangerous than the actual drug. Street buyers prefer to buy from known drug dealers as a guarantee of product and quality.

Untouchables: Drugs and Police Corruption

Temptation is everywhere. Given the prevalence of drug dealing and the fact that drug dealers hold hundreds and sometimes thousands of dollars in cash, police officers routinely face the opportunity for quick and illegal personal gain. Police could get away with stealing drugs or money, at least for a while. But robbed drug dealers can and will call Internal Affairs. And officers with criminal dealing will usually be ratted out by another criminal. Putting a dirty cop behind bars is as good of a get-out-of-jail card as exists.

I policed what is arguably the worst shift in the worst district in Baltimore and saw no police corruption. I know there are corrupt police officers. After three years on the street, one Eastern District officer stopped a man who drove his motorized scooter through a red light. The man had $6,300 in his pocket. The officer counted the money and allegedly returned $4,900 of it. The man called police to report the missing money and the officer was arrested and indicted on felony theft charges. One year later, these charges were dropped on condition that the officer resign from the police department and agree not to work in law enforcement again. When a cop is dirty, there is inevitably a drugs connection. Over a few beers after work, the subject of the drug squad came up. An older cop warned me to, "Stay away from drugs [in your dealings as a cop]. They'll just get you in trouble in the long run."

Incidents do happen, but the *police culture* is not corrupt. Though overall police integrity is very high, some will never be convinced. But out of personal virtue, internal investigation stings, or monetary calculations, the majority— the vast majority—of police officers are clean. A greater problem is that high-arrest officers push the boundaries of consent searches and turn pockets inside-out. Illegal (and legal) searches are almost always motivated by a desire to find drugs. In the academy, an officer warned the class, "Corruption starts six months to a year after you're out of the academy. When you're on the streets and you start shaking down drug dealers because they're worthless shits." Similarly a sergeant explained:

> You'll get out there, thinking you can make a difference. Then you get frustrated: a dealer caught with less than twenty-five pieces will be considered personal use. . . . Or you go to court and they take his word over yours. You're a cop and you're saying you saw something! . . . After it happens to you, you don't care. It's your job to bring him there [to court]. What happens after that is their problem. You can't take this job personal! Drugs were here before you were. And they'll be here long after you're

gone. Don't think you can change that. I don't want you leaving here thinking everybody living in this neighborhood is bad, does drugs. Many [cops] start beating people, thinking they deserve it.

Police officers are often in position to hold various amounts of drugs and money. Legally seized drugs and money are kept in one's pockets (carefully separated from personal belongings) before being taken to the station house and submitted in the proper fashion. Officers have to be careful to not make *honest* mistakes. They could put something in the wrong pocket. Something could fall out of a pocket. The night gets busy and they might forget to submit. Before each shift, police officers search the squad car cars for anything left behind.

Many residents, after repeated calls to police about drug dealers, assume that officers are either incorrigibly corrupt or completely apathetic:

I understand what you [police] deal with. But you got to understand. People see police drive right by the dealers, don't even get out of the car. Or they [police] got them [dealers] with their legs spread [being searched]. Who's to say you ain't taking a little something on the side? You can't have drugs on this scale without somebody letting it happen.

Police discount such accusations:

People get bad ideas from the media or from criminals that we're corrupt or brutal. But we're not. Or they refuse to think that their son could be involved with drugs. They want the corner cleared, but if we pick up their son it must be the racist cops picking on him because he's black. And with the amount of drugs you've got in this area, of course they aren't going to like police because we're trying to lock them up. Too many people here are pro-criminal.

Even financially, it pays to be straight. A New York City police officer explained:

My pension is worth between one and two million dollars. I'd have to be a fool to risk that for $100, even $1,000. I'll tell you when I'll be corrupt: the day I walk into a room piled with drugs, five million dollars in cash, and everybody dead. For five million, I'd do it. I'd leave the drugs and take the cash.

Some officers enter the police department corrupt. Others fall on their own free will. Still others may have an isolated instance of corruption in an otherwise honest career. But there is no natural force pulling officers from a free cup of coffee toward shaking down drug dealers. Police can omit superfluous facts from a police report without later perjuring themselves in court. Working unapproved security overtime does not lead to a life in the mob. Officers can take a cat nap at 4 AM and never abuse medical leave.[27] There is no slope. If anything, corruption is more like a Slip 'N Slide. You can usually keep your footing, but it's the drugs that make everything so damn slippery.

Stop Snitching

While the police see good communication between the public and the police as essential to fighting crime, relations are quite poor. This shouldn't be surprising. Drug users are criminal. If they want to stay out of jail, they and those who care for them have every reason to be wary of police. One officer complained: "Nobody here will talk to police. Half the public hates us. The other half is scared to talk to us. I would be, too. But we can't do anything without the public. They know who's dirty and who's not. They know who's shooting who. We don't know. They live here. We just drive around in big billboards. How are we supposed to see anything? The public doesn't understand that nothing will ever go to court if nobody talks. We can only do so much. As long as nobody ever sees anything, things aren't going to change." Police cannot base their testimony, or even a legal stop, on the claims of an anonymous call from a citizen.

The desire to remain anonymous comes from a combination of common sense and fear. Yet our system of justice depends on the willingness of victims and witnesses to testify. The Sixth Amendment says, "In all criminal prosecutions, the accused shall enjoy the right . . . to be confronted with the witnesses against him." No witness means no conviction. The "stop snitching" phenomenon compounds problem. Witness protection is minimal, and even when offered it is often turned down. Relocation is impractical when it involves moving away from home, family, friends, and babysitters.

The idea that "snitches get stitches" is not new, having roots going back at least to the Mob's code of Omerta. But wearing T-shirts to a criminal trial with "stop snitching" printed in a red stop sign is a relatively new fashion statement. The campaign's rise to prominence and the public's awareness of the snitching issue grew largely out of basketball star Carmelo Anthony's cameo appearance in a 2004 amateur Baltimore DVD called *Stop Fucking Snitching*. The video was in part a reaction to increased police success in "flipping" low-level drug suspects. In 2000, Baltimore detectives were instructed to interrogate all arrested drug suspects. Minor offenders could potentially gain their freedom with useful information about guns, murders, or major drug dealers.

The DVD is an often amusing but too long and poorly edited collection of street-corner bravado. A motley collection of self-proclaimed thugs rap, smoke weed, flash guns, and flaunt money. Snitches are named and threatened. Two corrupt police officers were outed as being "in the game." The Baltimore Police Department made a short video in response to *Stop Fucking Snitching* called "Keep Talking." In the end, many of the people featured in the video were arrested. The two named officers were arrested and convicted by a jury that did not believe their testimony that they were only playing by the informal rules of the narcotics game.

Yet overall, the significance of the stop snitching video is probably overblown. Quite simply, it's nothing new in the 'hood. The distinction between those "in the game" and "civilians" has never been clear. In October 2002, the Dawson home on Oliver Street was firebombed, killing both parents and their five children. A drug dealer was angry because he believed that Mr. and Mrs. Dawson kept calling the police.[28] When witnesses get killed, people don't need a video or T-shirt to tell them to keep quiet.

New or not, the impact of silence is hugely detrimental to police and prosecutors. Even without personal risks, there is little incentive to testify. Nobody gains though interaction with the criminal justice system. You don't get paid for it; there is no guarantee that testimony will result in conviction and jail time; and after the second or third postponement, a sense of civic duty usually fades. The hassles of court—passing through metal detectors, wasted days, milling around crowds of criminals—combined with practical matters such as work and childcare make it far easier, even smarter, to see nothing, hear nothing, and mind your own business.

Police Perspective

Because of these problems and the "victimless" nature of drug crimes, most drug arrests are at the initiative of police officers. On one occasion, while driving slowly through a busy drug market early one morning, I saw dozens of African American addicts milling about while a smaller group of young men and boys were waiting to sell. Another officer in our squad had just arrested a drug addict for loitering. I asked my partner, "What's the point of arresting people for walking down the street?" He replied: "Because everybody walking down the street is a criminal. In Canton or Greektown [middle-class neighborhoods] people are actually going somewhere. How many people here aren't dirty? ['None.'] It's drugs. . . . If all we can do is lock 'em up for loitering, so be it."

Police have diverse opinions toward the drug problem. I asked my sergeant if it was more effective to arrest drug addicts or to remain on and patrol the street to temporarily disrupt drug markets. He surprised me by choosing the former:

> Arresting someone sends a better message. Locking up junkies makes a difference. This squad used to have more arrests than five of the districts. We used to go out every

night and just make arrest runs as a squad. Start with six cars, like a train. Fill one up, then you have five cars. Continue until you're out of cars. At 1 AM, everybody on a drug corner is involved with drugs. We locked them up for loitering. Got lots of drugs, a few weapons, too. After a few weeks, everything was quiet. Eventually it got so that we had to poach from other districts. We ran out of people to arrest. You think the neighbors didn't like that?

Police are defined by arrests, so an arrest-based approach toward the drug problem is popular. Mocking a much disparaged comment attributed to a former commissioner, one officer said, "We're not 'social workers with guns.' We're PO-lice. . . . We're supposed to be locking up the drug addicts, not sending them for referral." Another officer simply said: "I lock up junkies." He explained:

Some people consider that a bullshit lockup. But fuck 'em. I don't see them locking up Al Capone. You bring your skanky white ass into East Baltimore and I'll send you right to C.B.I.F. [jail]. If I lock somebody up before they buy drugs, that's one less chance that they're going to get robbed. One less chance they're going to get shot. One less chance they're going to OD right before shift change. If everybody locked up all the junkies, eventually they'd give up. Plus I love [the overtime money from] court!

Another officer explained how a high-arrest strategy would make the streets safer:

I'll tell you how. Go out there and lock everybody up. If you're standing on the corner, you go to jail. If you've got drugs on you, you stay there [in jail]. We could clear up these streets. But people go crazy as soon as you lock up their baby. Some people out here actually do have jobs. And they want the corner cleared until they realize that it's their son standing out there.

Other police officers, however, questioned the benefit of repeatedly arresting addicts:

Locking up junkies isn't going to do it. They've got to go after the kingpin. The big man. The man with the moolah. But there's too much power up there. You go high enough and you never know who you're going to find. You think it's just here in Baltimore? They don't grow poppies in East Baltimore.

Another officer said:

They've got to keep people in jail. I'd like to see some of that "three-strikes-you're-out" here. We keep locking up the same people over and over again. And they get right out. They don't care if they go to jail: three hots and a cot. The whole system is joke. What do you expect? People don't change.

A veteran sergeant proposed raising the risk of drug-related deaths as a means of scaring addicts into quitting:

You really want to know? I've got a plan, but you won't like this. What you've got to do is put bad drugs out there. Make people get sick. Kill a few. The only way a junkie is ever going to kick the habit is if he's afraid he's going to die. If every time somebody was shooting up, there was a good change they'd die? You'd solve the drug problem in a month. Or at least people wouldn't start.

People are dying now. You've seem 'em overdose. And it's good for business because all the other junkies want some of that "good shit."

Nobody believes that victory in the drug war is imminent. Nor do police believe that current tactics can do anything other than maintain the status quo. Some police blame the Constitution for limiting police officers' ability to arrest drug criminals: "Yeah, I think the Constitution should be unamended. If we could stop whoever we wanted, there would be a lot less crime. Criminals have all the rights. That's why they call it the *criminal* justice system." Many police offer some variations of this.

The majority of police do not want drug laws softened. One sergeant told me, "Look, we're out there doing what we can. Should we just throw in the towel? Legalization would send the wrong message. We don't legalize murder just because we can't stop it. If we weren't out there, the problem would be a lot worse." In survey data, one-fifth of officers agree that possession of small amounts of marijuana should be legal.[29] A smaller minority supports complete legalization of all drugs. This support comes more from a libertarian philosophy of limited government than a belief in harm reduction or effective policy. As one office put it, "Fuck. I'd just legalize it all. I don't think it's the state's business telling people what they can and can't do anyway. Legalize it, regulate it, tax it. And then I'd go home and smoke a big doobie."

It may seem incongruous for police officers to see the futility of drug enforcement and simultaneously promote increased drug enforcement. But for many, the drug war is a moral issue and retreat would "send the message": "It's a crusade for me. My brother and a cousin died from heroin overdoses. I know that on some level it's a choice they made. But there was also a dealer pushing it on them. I want to go out and get these drug dealers."

Another officer was more explicit: "You've got to see it [drugs] as evil. What do you think? It's good? When we're out there, risking our lives, we're on the side of good. Drugs are evil. It's either that or seeing half the people in the Eastern [District] as being evil. I like to think that I'm helping good people fight evil. That's what I'd like to think."

As long as drugs are illegal, someone on the corner will deal drugs. When police confront the public drug dealers, police will almost always win the individual battle. But there is no hope that the current system of policing will let us win the war on drugs. The failure of police to eliminate street-level drug dealing is nothing new. Berkeley professor and chief of police August Vollmer said it seventy years ago: "One notorious peddler stood on a corner and waited until his customer dropped money near a telephone pole. He picked it up, and one of his agents put the drug wanted, as indicated by the amount of money, in a crevice in the same telephone pole. Where money is taken by one person and the package is inserted by another, conviction is difficult if not impossible."[30]

The attitudes of police and criminal are largely controlled by a desire to protect their turf while avoiding unnecessary interactions. On each call for service, drug dealers generally do not wish to provoke the police and most police officers are not looking for adventure. At night, curfew violations can be enforced on minors. Open containers can be cited. People can be arrested for some minor charge. But arrests take officers off the street and leave the drug corner largely unpoliced while the prisoner is booked. Nothing police officers do will disrupt the drug trade longer than it takes drug dealers to walk around the block and recongregate. One officer expressed this dilemma well: "We can't do anything. Drugs were here before I was born and they're going to be here after I die. All they pay us to do is herd junkies."

CHAPTER 5

911 Is a Joke

It makes about as much sense to have police patrol
routinely in cars to fight crime as it does to have
firemen patrol routinely in firetrucks to fight fire.

—*Professor Carl Klockars*

A fourteen-year-old holds six orange-topped vials of
crack cocaine in his pocket.[1] He sits with two older
friends, ages sixteen and seventeen, on the marble stoop of
an East Baltimore row home at 1:00 AM.[2] It is a cool and
quiet school night. All three wear white T-shirts, baggy
jeans below their waists, and brown Timberland shoes. All
three have criminal records.

A run-down car drives slowly down a residential street
lined with both well kept and boarded-up row-homes. The
sixteen-year-old gets up, holds up his pants with his right
hand, and motions with his left to hail a "hack," an unlicensed taxi. The car slows down in front of him and the
driver asks if they're "up." The youth responds, "Yeah."
The driver says he wants some "ready" and hands the
sixteen-year-old a $20 bill. The sixteen-year-old returns to
the stoop and the fourteen-year-old then jogs to the car and
gives the driver a vial of crack cocaine.

The car drives away and the three return to their original positions. The oldest, legally still a juvenile at age seventeen, has been arrested eight times for a variety of crimes:
three times for loitering, once each for failure to appear
in court, destruction of property, auto theft, possession of

cocaine, and a handgun violation. He takes the money and adds it to a small roll of tens and twenties.

Across the street an elderly man looks through a darkened curtain. Without turning on the lights, he dials 911. Within a ring, an operator answers his call and says, "911. Your call is being recorded. This is operator 5627. What is your emergency?" The man tells the operator, "Those three hoppers are out selling drugs again on the 1800 block of East Eager." When prompted for a description, he says, "They all got on white T-shirts and jeans." He emphatically states that he wishes to remain anonymous and hangs up.

The 911 operator types the information into her computer and it is relayed electronically to the Eastern District dispatcher. A few minutes later the police dispatcher hails the post officer responsible for the block and says: "CDS [controlled dangerous substance, i.e., drugs], 1800 block of East Eager. Three number-one [black] males dealing drugs on the stoop. White T-shirts and jeans. No further [description]. [Caller wishes to remain] Anonymous."

Fifteen minutes later, a marked police car driven by a rookie police officer drives slowly up the street. The block is empty except for the three youths.

I stopped in front of them and rolled down the passenger-side window. I looked at all three, but my attention was on the youngest.

"How old is he?" I ask.
"Who, me?" the youngest youth replies.
"How old are you?"
"Seventeen," says the fourteen-year-old.
"Where do you live?"
"Up the street."

"Where do you live?" I ask more harshly.

"2086 Biddle."

"Perhaps one of these two gentlemen will escort you home right now?"

The seventeen-year-old's face makes a quizzical expression and I say:

"Bounce!" The seventeen-year-old stands up with the fourteen-year-old.

"Any of you have ID?" I ask.

"Naw," the older two reply.

"Who lives here?"

"Me," says the sixteen-year-old.

"Go home. If I see any of you out here tonight, I'll lock your ass up."

All three begin to walk away. I turn my gaze toward the sixteen-year-old: "Where are you going? You live here. If you can't open that door, you're going to Central Booking. Go inside."

The sixteen-year-old begins to protest, but instead says, "Aw'ite" [all right].

He walks up the five marble steps, opens the unlocked door, and enters the house. The other two walk away. I fill out a line on my daily run sheet and key up my radio, "Three-adam-twenty-three."

"Twenty-three," the dispatcher replies.

"Frank-no [call abated] for Eager [Street]. Anything else in Sector Two?"

"Frank-no. Ten-four. Twenty-three, can you back up [unit] twenty-two? Domestic assault. 1501 Preston. A Lawanda says she was hit by baby's father. No further [description]. Twenty-two, you copy?"

"Ten-four."

I head to the next call. In twenty minutes, the two older boys have returned to their position on the row-home stoop. The anonymous caller who called 911 is sure to call again. Because each call for drug activity is considered a separate incident by the police department, repeated calls for the same group of people are recorded as a series of resolved incidents rather than a continuation of a single problem. Because there is little police officers can do on a drug call to solve the problem, officers generally welcome these calls as "easy." And as most drug crimes are victimless and most calls are anonymous, there is nobody to placate, and usually no paperwork.

Police departments are committed to responding to every citizen's request for police service, so the primary job of the patrol officer is to answer 911 and 311 calls for service.[3] More than any tactical strategy or mandate from the police administration, citizens' telephone calls control the majority of police services. The emphasis on radio calls means that in busy districts, officers can do little other than answer dispatched calls for service. A system allowing all citizens unlimited and equal access to police services is, at its core, very democratic. The reality, however, is anything but. Police service is not unlimited. Access must inevitably be controlled. Police respond to the most overt manifestation of a problem or to the location at which one citizen, justified or not, demands repeated police presence.[4]

The advent of patrol cars, telephones, two-way radios, "scientific" police management, social migration, and social science theories on the "causes" of crime converged in the late 1950s. Before then, police had generally followed a "watchman" approach: each patrol officer was given the responsibility to police a geographic area.[5] In the decades after World War II, motorized car patrol replaced foot patrol as the standard method of policing. Improved technology allowed citizens to call police and have their complaints dispatched to police through two-way radios in squad cars. Car patrol was promoted over foot patrol as a cost-saving move justified by increased "efficiency."[6]

Those who viewed police as provocative and hostile to the public applauded reduced police presence and discretion. Controlled by the central dispatch, police could respond to the desires of the community rather than enforce their own "arbitrary" concepts of "acceptable" behavior. Police officers, for their part, enjoyed the comforts of the automobile and the prestige associated with new technology. Citizens, rather than being encouraged to maintain community standards, were urged to stay behind locked doors and call 911.

Car patrol eliminated the neighborhood police officer. Police were pulled off neighborhood beats to fill cars. But motorized patrol—the cornerstone of urban policing—has no effect on crime rates, victimization, or public satisfaction.[7] Lawrence Sherman was an early critic of telephone dispatch and motorized patrol, noted, "The rise of telephone dispatch transformed both the method and purpose of patrol. Instead of *watching to prevent* crime, motorized police patrol became a process of merely *waiting to respond* to crime."[8]

A quick response time became an end in itself rather than a means to crime prevention. In order to respond quickly, police are pressured to be "in service," ready to receive dispatched calls. Parked alone in the middle of an empty parking lot—the ominous police car and the long walk discourage pesky citizens from approaching—a police officer is considered "in service." When dealing with people—the essence of the job, some might argue—police are considered "out of service." David Bayley explains this police prime directive:

> Despite what police say, the prime directive of patrolling is to be available rather than to respond adequately to the myriad calls for service. For police managers, therefore, patrol officers are "working" when they are simply cruising around. . . . Police forces must store capacity, and they do so in patrol. For patrol officers as well as for commanders, claims of being busy are a way of disguising the invisible burden of always being ready.[9]

Because patrol officers spend most of their work-day sitting in a police car or driving around, officers develop a car-centered method of policing their post. Officers learn most of their knowledge of an area through the window of a patrol car. Even in an area where most crime occurs on the sidewalk and most residents do not own a car (much less drive to work), officers are more attuned to potholes and stoplight timing than to street crime and quality-of-life issues. The high volume and low content of 911 calls further discourages any routine nonconfrontational interactions between the police and the public.

The disproved theory behind car patrol, still taught in today's police academies and criminal justice textbooks, is known as the "three Rs." The first "R" is "random patrol," police drive in nonfixed patterns to create the illusion of police "omnipresence." This stands in direct contrast to the older idea of police walking in a fixed and regular beat.

The Kansas City Preventive Patrol Experiment proved this:

During 1972 and 1973 a year-long experiment was conducted in Kansas City, Missouri, to test the effects of preventive patrol. The idea for the study originated within the Kansas City Police Department, and the experiment was designed and carried out with the assistance of the Police Foundation. Fifteen patrol beats were included in the study: five were control beats with normal levels of preventive patrol; five were proactive beats with 2–3 times the normal levels of patrol; and five were reactive beats, with no preventative patrol. It is important to realize that patrol units would enter the reactive beats to answer calls whenever requested. After handling calls, however, these patrol units would vacate the reactive beats and do their patrolling in other areas. . . . When the data were analyzed, no significant differences were found on any of the indicators between the control, proactive, and reactive beats.[10]

In debunking random patrol and omnipresence, the Kansas City study cast doubt on the previously unquestioned faith in motorized random patrol as an effective and essential means of policing. Yet the impact of the Kansas City report, despite being one of the most heralded scientific police studies, was negligible.

The second of the three "Rs" is "rapid response," the theory that a quick police response to the scene of a crime will result in the greater apprehension of criminals. As rapid police response is not designed to *prevent* crime, its failure to do so should come as no surprise. For fire trucks and ambulances, the benefit of rapid response is obvious: quick response saves lives. Rapid police response, though it may seem counter intuitive, has almost no effect on the odds that a criminal will be caught. Even instantaneous police response would be ineffective as the vast majority of the time most 911 callers—whether by necessity, choice, or confusion—wait until a suspect is gone before reporting a crime.[11]

It is not the victims' fault that police receive very few "in progress" calls. Even if victims were to respond "correctly" or a third-party calls police while a crime is in progress, dispatch takes time. The 911 operator must answer the call, gather the relevant information, and enter it into a computer. This information is then sent to the relevant police dispatcher. The dispatcher then finds time to dispatch the call to a police officer. More often than not, even if police just happen to be in the right place at the right time, callers have been waiting for five, ten, even twenty minutes. And if police do not arrive within one minute of a crime, rapid police response has virtually no effect.[12] Even if police *could* respond instantaneously, they wouldn't want to. Best to let people tire themselves out or resolve their petty problems on their own.

Yet despite the basic failure of reactive policing, car-based patrol is popular on many levels: Radio cars provide a means to account for and control officers; police officers like being sheltered from the street in the comparative comfort of a car; and police administrators generally find it easier to focus on response time than crime prevention. And the public loves the illusion of picking up the phone and having a police officer magically appear.

The third of the three "Rs" is "reactive investigation," the effective working of the criminal justice system to "solve" crimes and provide deterrence against future crimes. While investigation is rightfully a key part of police work in solving crimes, the public's beliefs in these techniques is hugely inflated. The O. J. Simpson trial raised the bar too high for the preservation of chaotic crime scenes. And TV shows, most notably *CSI: Crime Scene Investigation*, portray a faith in technology that, when not absolute fiction, is science-fiction for most police departments. Crimes get solved because people talk. Call them rats, finks, stoolies, confidential informants, cooperating witnesses, or good citizens, it's the good old-fashioned snitch that solves crime. Science and technology have a long way to go. And solving a homicide is much less important than preventing a murder in the first place.

Bullshit Calls

While most people don't call 911 at all, others call 911 daily. Police in Baltimore's Eastern District handled 113,205 calls for service in 2000, or about two-and-one-half calls per resident per year.[13] (See table 5.1.) This is roughly four times the national average.[14] The total number of primary calls is approximately one call per hour per patrol officer. But officers respond formally and informal as back-up to many more calls. The frequency of calls per officer increases when other officers are "detailed," "out of service," or otherwise unable to take calls. And call volume is not evenly dispersed throughout the day. Noon to 2 AM is generally busy while 3 AM to 7 AM is generally slow.

TABLE 5.1
Annual Police Calls for Service in Baltimore's
Eastern District

Category of Dispatched Call for Service	Category as Percentage (n) of All Calls
All Calls for Service	100% (113,205)
Drugs	25.6% (28,959)
Disorderly	10.5% (11,874)
"Other"	8.8% (9,953)
Alarms	8.3% (9,353)
Common Assault	6.9% (7,865)
911 No Voice	5.6% (6,341)
Larceny	3.8% (4,346)
Family Disturbance	2.9% (3,277)
Auto Accident	2.6% (2,990)
Burglary	2.3% (2,639)
Armed Person	1.9% (2,168)
Destruction of Property	1.8% (2,059)
Aggravated Assault	1.4% (1,580)
Selected Other Categories	
Gunshots	0.9% (980)
Stolen Auto	0.9% (969)

TABLE 5.1 (*continued*)

Assault, Shooting	0.3% (324)
Assault, Cutting	0.3% (312)
Rape	0.1% (120)
Carjacking	0.04% (48)
Not Listed Above	15.1% (17,048)

Percentage (n) of Dispatched Calls With:	
No Need for Police Response	38.9% (44,003)
Some Police Service Provided	35.4% (40,093)
Crime Committed or Call Requires a Written Report	25.7% (29,109)

Source: Baltimore City Police Department, 2000. Data recoded by author. Moskos 2007.

Before the 911 system was introduced, citizens in need of police service found a police officer or called the local police station. *All* calls for service required a written report. After 911 was introduced, requests for police service skyrocketed and police were overwhelmed by report writing. The system was changed so that today only arrests, crimes with victims, and domestic-related incidents require written reports.

Thirty-nine percent of calls to which police respond require no police response Police call these unfounded calls "bogus" or "bullshit."[15] While the definition of a "bullshit" call is somewhat flexible, one officer defined a "bullshit call" as:

> Something we shouldn't be there for. "Bullshit" is people call police, but then get mad that you show up. Or when you show up, and they make shit up. Bullshit is any junkie who wastes my time because they got burnt [ripped-off on a drug deal] and say, "I was robbed." Or some bitch who don't get paid and says, "I was raped!" Everything out here is bullshit. Half the CDS [drug] calls are bullshit . . . What can we do about it? People want their rights. People here just want their drugs, their "hair-ron" [heroin], some malt liquor, and a "little some'm' some'm' " [something something, i.e., sex]. We just get in the way.

While all unfounded calls are considered "bullshit," not all "bullshit" calls are unfounded. Legitimate but minor calls most often achieve their bovine descriptive because of an uncooperative victim or the inability of the officer to "do anything." Many victims of even violent crime are uncooperative with police due to fear of or friendship with the suspect. Other victims simply—and wisely, if they are wanted—choose to avoid interaction with an ineffective criminal justice system. It is not unusual for crime victims to be uncooperative and, for example, not even reveal their name.

Illegitimate calls stem from a variety of sources. A large percentage of calls are simply fictitious: people use 911 to harass enemies, to draw police away from an area, and to

make prank phone calls. Calls that require no police response include a complainant who cannot be located; a
location that does not exist; a call reporting that an un-
armed stranger at a bus stop is armed; a burglary at a location at which there is no building; a false report of a
man shot; or a person, usually a child, who dials 911 and
hangs up. As a category, 90 percent of these "911
hangups"—6 percent of all dispatched calls—are completely unfounded.[16]

In general, officers are surprisingly good at determining
the validity of a call from the sparse information received
from the dispatcher:

> There's lots of clues, even when they [dispatchers] barely
> tell us anything. First, there's the location. Small-time
> robberies or rapes at drug corners are bullshit. People
> getting burnt [ripped-off by drug dealers] and what not.
> A real shooting will get lots of calls. If you're harassing
> drug dealers and one call comes in for a shooting a few
> blocks away, you know it's bullshit. Other calls you know
> are legit. There aren't too many fake cuttings. If you get
> a call for a cutting, good chance you're going to see some
> blood. Assaults are usually bullshit. [Calls for] burglaries,
> destruction of properties, stolen autos—well, not always
> stolen cars—but in general they're legit . . . Other times
> you get information from the dispatcher and know there's
> nothing you can do. Or should do. Somebody can't raise
> their kid? What the hell am I supposed to do? I ain't
> baby's father.

The same officer expressed frustration with the 911
system:

I don't know why they have us responding to calls we can't do anything about. "He said, she said." All we do is tell them to go to a court commissioner. We can't do shit if we didn't see it. But they still send an officer. That way it's on us [the patrol officer] and not on them [the department].

Drug Calls

Drug calls are one-fourth of all dispatched calls (citywide, excluding the Eastern District, drug calls are approximately 7.5 percent of all calls).[17] But most calls have some drug-related angle. A disorderly call involves disorderly drug dealers. An assault is over a drug deal gone bad. A murder is between two drug dealers. Anonymous calls about a group of youths dealing don't help police officers. Police already know the hot drug corners:

> What's the point of telling us there's CDS on 700 Port, or Madeira and Chase, or Wolfe and Eager? No shit. Either you let us jack everybody up [stop and search people on the street], lock everybody up just for being there, or you live with it.

> We're not going to stop drug dealing. Look at all the junkies around. They're gonna buy! But people call 911 and we drive by. Ninety percent of this job is clearing corners, harassing junkies, and paperwork. What's left? I got to eat lunch and take a dump, too. How much worse would the city be if I just turned off the radio and did my job? I guarantee you I could do a better job if it weren't for Alice [the dispatcher] always shouting in my ear.

We can't get shit done because calls are always coming in. How many are really "in progress"? Five percent? How many are innocent victims? None.

As police must appear at each calls request, the quality of these responses plummets as the quantity increases. For drug corners, more often than not, this means having the group walk around the block.

Police officers usually know whether a group of suspects is actively, occasionally, or never involved with selling drugs. Some residents, often elderly, believe that all youths, particularly those who present themselves as "thug" or "ghetto," are involved with drug dealing. If police respond to a call for a group of people known not to be criminals, police will approach politely. If the group seems honestly surprised to see the police, they may be given some presumption of innocence. An officer could ask if everything is all right or if the group knows any reason why the police would have been called. If the suspects are unknown to a police officer, the group's response to police attention is used as the primary clue. Even with a presumption of guilt, a group that walks away without being prompted will generally be allowed to disperse. If a group of suspects challenges police authority through language or demeanor, the officer is compelled to act. This interaction is so ritualized that it resembles a dance.

If temporary dispersal of a group is the goal, the mere arrival of a patrol car should be all that is needed. Every additional step, from stopping the car to exiting the car to questioning people on the street, known as a "field interview," is a form of escalation on the part of the police officer.

Aware of the symbolism and ritual of such actions, police establish a pattern in which a desired outcome is achieved quickly, easily, and with a minimum of direct confrontation. Rarely is there any long-term impact.

When a police officer slows his or her car down in front of the individuals, the suspects know the officer is there for them and not just passing through on the way to other business. If a group of suspects does not disperse when an officer "rolls up," the officer will stop the car and stare at the group. A group may ignore the officer's look or engage the officer in a stare-off, known in police parlance as "eye fucking." This officer's stare serves the dual purpose of scanning for contraband and weapons and simultaneously declaring dominance over turf.

An officer will initiate, often aggressively, conversation from the car and ask where the suspects live and if they have any identification. Without proof of residence, the suspects will be told to leave and threatened with arrest. If the group remains or reconvenes, they are subject to a loitering arrest. Police officers always assert their right to control public space. Every drug call to which police respond—indeed all police dealings with social or criminal misbehavior—will result in the suspect's arrest, departure, or deference.

Policing such a neighborhood requires a certain amount of aggressiveness. The code of the street allows one to avoid confrontation, but the code also states that to enter and back down from a conflict is a loss of face.[18] Nobody wants to be "punked," least of the all the police.[19] Police play by these street rules with the assumption that any sign of weakness on their part will make future interactions much more difficult and dangerous. Police, quite simply, cannot afford to lose confrontations. I never had to provoke or initiate violence on the street. But I couldn't help but wonder if the compliance I received (I purposefully avoid calling it "respect") was due, as I like to think, to my excellent policing and interpersonal skills or the simple fact that a previous post officer had beat the crap out of some guy who questioned his authority.

While police officers rarely discharge their guns on duty, police shootings (police being shot) and police-involved shootings (police shooting a suspect) are not rare. Between 1999 and 2007, four police officers were killed by gunfire and many more shot and wounded. In 1999, when I went on the force, Baltimore police shot thirty-two people, killing five of them, a typical annual number. In the first five months of 2007, five people died after being shot by police, four with gunfire and fifth with a Taser. Despite these high levels of violence, most line-of-duty injuries and deaths result from all-too-frequent car crashes. Despite this, many police officers refuse to wear their seatbelts.

Interactions vary depending on the police officer involved. One officer said, "You can't just roll by and tell people to leave the corner and then come back and arrest them. You wait for them to leave. And if they don't, you get out of your car." Al Capone had it half right when he said, "You can get more with a kind word and a gun than you can with a kind word alone." But a better phrasing for police would be that you can get more with a kind word and a gun than you can with a *gun* alone.

Some officers, due to time constraints, laziness, or fear, will seldom get out of their car. To residents, officers who remain in their cars on a drug call seem lazy or corrupt—a "hump," in police parlance. For a police officer, however, remaining in the patrol car can be entirely reasonable: "I'm not going to get out of the car unless I have to. If I get out, somebody's going to get locked up. Look, we get how many calls for CDS an hour? I don't have to get out of the car just to tell someone to take a walk. I want there to be impact if I get out. We're not allowed to hit people anymore, so I want me walking up to them to have the same effect. If they know I mean business, they'll do what I want without me even stopping the car. That's not being a hump. That's good policing. That's respect."

On a slow shift, officers may be more proactive. Some officers enjoy "pooping and snooping," hiding with binoculars in nearby weeds, a vacant building, or the Hopkins's Hospital parking garage to conduct surveillance of a drug corner. Young and eager police will jump out on suspects and stop and search—"jack up"—an addict or dealer and the immediate area for weapons and drugs. This can be an easy way to make an arrest: "Unless it's a busy night, I'm going to jack-up whoever I can. They may not all have drugs on them. But nine times out of ten, one of them is dirty. It may not even be what they're dealing. Maybe just a blunt [marijuana in a cigar] for 'personal consumption.' "

The legality of the initial stop depends entirely on the officer's ability to articulate reasonable suspicion. Though many drug searches are illegal extensions of frisks, drug suspects, whether believing that drugs are well hidden or that acquiescence is the path of least resistance, consent to searches far more often than most outsiders (and judges) believe possible.

A drug call can be resolved in a few seconds or, with surveillance and investigation, can take upward of an hour. Such a range gives patrol officers the ability to "sit on the call," remain "out of service," and not receive other dispatched calls. With this block of time, officers may finish paperwork, go to the bathroom, eat an uninterrupted lunch, or simply avoid answering "bad" calls for another officer who is also trying to avoid taking calls. "Bad" calls, such as suspected child abuse or DOA (dead body), involve more time commitment, paperwork, or unforgettably horrible smells.

When sitting on a call, conscientious officers will come back in service for any call on their post, an ideal, believed to be disappearing, known as "post integrity." If no officer is in service and available to answer calls, the dispatcher may assign the call to their sergeant. This is a good way to get officers back in service. Sergeants are not supposed to answer calls for service and squads generally pride themselves on being able to handle their business. There are times, however, when the entire district goes "down," i.e., working and therefore considered out of service. On these rare occasions— usually the result of being short a few officers and having two or three unrelated shootings at the same time—units from other districts can be brought in to answer calls.

In a throwback to the past when the dispatcher placed index cards in a police officer's box, present-day officers ask for backed-up calls on their post to be put in their "box." In the precomputer days, these nonemergency calls would wait until the post officer was free to deal with them. Computers and 911 dispatch, however, have taken discretion away from the dispatcher and the police officer. The perverse internal logic of rapid response demands that even nonemergency calls be quickly assigned to any available officer, even if that officer lacks knowledge and experience with the address or people involved.

Even when there aren't many calls coming in, the *possibility* of receiving a call prevents officers from doing foot patrol, in-depth investigations, or any activity that may cause an officer to stray too far from the patrol car. An officer with over thirty-years of experience talked about the greater knowledge he had before patrol was car based and dispatch controlled: "Back in the old days [the late 1960s and 1970s], there was such a thing as post integrity. You were out there walking around and people knew you. Things were different. You [police] could get away with anything. . . . But that's just the way things were. We had a lot of fun. But we also knew what was going on. People talked to us and trusted us. Well, some of them." Police isolated in squad cars will not know the community. Today foot patrol is most often a form of punishment. And no police officer is ever promoted to beat cop.

While the public generally favors increased foot patrol, the opposition to foot patrol in the police organization is strong. A car is comfortable, your feet don't get tired, you can listen to the radio, talk to your partner in private, stay warm and dry, and it's easier to avoid problem people until *after* they commit a serious crime. Then you simply arrest them. Yet dealing with problem people *before* they commit a crime, though perhaps undesirable, is a police officer's job. This isn't possible in an era of rapid-response.

With fewer cars and a deemphasis of rapid response, police officers could better mitigate the problems of the drug corner. A better system would require police dispatchers or police officers to exercise professional judgment and separate legitimate from illegitimate calls (and affirm current legal protection for good-faith police errors). Free from the tyranny of dispatch, officers could focus on quality rather than quantity of response. Walking the beat, officers would learn their area and gain the trust of more citizens. Freeing police resources would make response more consistent and reliable, even faster, for the very rare serious crime in progress. By not promising (and usually failing to deliver) rapid response to all calls, patrol officers could focus on the quality-of-life issues that concern residents and the broken windows characteristic of a neighborhood out of control.

Such a system would not be perfect, but it could be demonstrably better than the status quo. It could be tested in an area as small as one sector covered by the dozen or so police officers already under the command of one sergeant. Experienced patrol officers would respond to all calls on their post. These officers would be free to walk their beat and use their discretion to solve local criminal problems. Nonemergency calls could be kept on an appointment basis. These officers, perhaps ironically, would still need access to rapid police response for backup. Inexperienced, lazy, or otherwise uncooperative officers could be placed in patrol cars to respond to legitimate emergency calls in progress and provide officer backup.

There are not enough police resources to emphasize both rapid response and any real alternative to a reactive, car-based patrol. The public that most needs police protection is already aware of the failure of 911 and police response; the rest of the public—the more influential and prominent citizens that generally defend the status quo and do not call for the police—need to be "unsold" on the necessity and inevitability of reactive patrol. Recognizing the failures and limitations of the status quo is the first step to better patrol: 911 calls dominate police far more than rapid response impacts crime or the drug trade.

CHAPTER 6

Under Arrest:
Discretion in the Ghetto

> All they want us to do is lock up junkies and not get
> complaints. It's always been a numbers game.
>
> —*A Baltimore City police officer*

I received the call for suspected physical child abuse. A
juvenile said he was beaten by his guardian and locked
out of the house. This "juvenile" was himself a father, a
tough seventeen-year-old who had been drinking. His name
was James and his fifty-two-year-old grandmother, Amelia,
was his legal guardian. James's mother bounced between
rehab and jail and, according to the guardian, played a very
minor role in her children's upbringing. As legal guardian,
Miss Amelia was responsible for James until his eighteenth
birthday, still a few months away. Until then, James had every legal right to be in that house.

Miss Amelia explained that James moved out about a
year ago, when he started selling drugs. James would occasionally get drunk, come home, threaten her, and demand
money. She hadn't seen him in weeks. This time she refused to let James in. After he called his grandmother a
bitch, she hit him and closed the door in his face. Legally
Miss Amelia is guilty of assault, physical child abuse, and
child neglect. She could also be held responsible for James's
underage drinking and general social and criminal misbehavior. Legally the guardian could be arrested and James
placed under the care of protective social services until

Miss Amelia can demonstrate adequate parenting skill, perhaps after completing some required anger management class.

Of course Miss Amelia was not arrested. In such a case, discretion trumps law. James was given a stern lecture and told to leave, stay away, and threatened with arrest if he ever touched his grandmother. But after he left, Miss Amelia was informed of some of the legal realities on James's side. She wanted to disown James but was advised it would take too long. The only real option was to wait for him to turn eighteen. If he came back she would just have to call police and hope for the best. To me, she apologized for James, "I tried the best I could. I did everything I could. But, Lord, it wasn't enough. . . . He didn't turn out right." She mentioned some of those she did raise right, one was in the army and many had regular jobs.

Policing, like all human action, involves discretion. Sometimes police discretion is legal, as when a driver is given a warning rather than a ticket. Other times, as in the case of the "abusive" grandmother, discretion may be extralegal. Such discretion is not only inevitable, it is good. Different police officers handle similar situations in different ways. In day-to-day police actions, the chain of command is a myth. A sergeant cannot be in active command of five units simultaneously. Ultimately we have to trust officers' discretion because we have no choice. Some officers are more physically dominant, others are better verbally; some rely on arrest, others on persuasion, still others on threats. While officers may believe that another officer handles certain situations poorly, the idea that officers should be allowed to make their own decisions is never in question. If these decisions are wrong, then the officers will face the legal, departmental, or physical consequences.

The vast majority of calls for service do not result in an arrest and the bulk of arrests are not felonies. For minor and nonviolent offenses, such as traffic citations and nonfelony arrests, police officers exercise a great deal of discretion. But for felony crimes—especially those involving victims and violence—police have relatively little arrest discretion. Felony arrests are largely a function of luck and an officer's ability to identify and locate a suspect. If a man is bleeding and a woman is holding a bloody knife yelling, "I cut that son of a bitch and I'd do it again," she will get arrested. If the suspect cannot be located, the patrol officer makes no arrest and hands the case over to a detective. For the most part, patrol officers stumble across felony arrests; officers cannot set out to lock up a violent felon. But in any given work shift an officer can decide to write five traffic tickets or lock up two low-level drug offenders.

Every situation has a primary officer, the officer who makes the call on what should happen, who should be told to go home, who if anybody should be locked up, and how the paperwork will be categorized. Formally the primary officer is the first officer to arrive on scene. Informally post integrity demands that the post officers takes over any call dispatched on their post. But any action you choose to take, necessary or not, is your responsibility. This is captured in the well-worn police phrase, "on-view, on-you."

In 1943, William Whyte was the first sociologist to describe what is now called police discretion. Building on Whyte and inspired by the Civil Rights Movement, the

legal community documented the "problem" of police discretion in the 1960s and declared it illegal, immoral, and in
violation of a democratic ethos.[1] In 1967, Egon Bittner was
the first to cast a positive light on police discretion, an underappreciated skill that allowed police to keep the peace
on skid-row. Law enforcement demands discretion. Every
statute on the books cannot and should not be enforced.
Departmental regulations say plenty about what police officers can and cannot do, but they offer little guidance as to
why and *how* a situation should be handled. For this, officers
rely on what they think is common sense, namely the law
tempered by experience, ethics, the norms of their colleagues and the community, and potential for court overtime pay.

Heads You Walk, Tails You Go: Discretionary Arrests

Though any minor charge will suffice, loitering is the most
widely used minor criminal charge in Baltimore. Loitering is
defined, in part, as "interfering, impeding, or hindering the
free passage of pedestrian or vehicular traffic after receiving
a warning."[2] In practice, loitering is failing to move when ordered to move by a police officer. The act of simply *being* is
also criminalized in the concept of a "drug-free zone." Drug-
free zones, defined by the city council, encompass a large
part of the Eastern District. In practice, "loitering in a drug-
free zone" is charged infrequently because an officer's arrest
report requires a listing of the drug-free zone's boundaries, a
burdensome addition of a little writing.

Only in high-drug areas do police officers make exten-
sive use of discretionary non-drug-related charges, such as
loitering. These arrests are very fickle, but invariably linked

to the drug game. One officer described an unorthodox approach he used very rarely: "Sometimes I'll flip a quarter for a loiterer. Tails he goes to jail and heads he doesn't. They'll be going, 'Heads! Yeeah!'" I asked if they ever fuss when the coin came up tails. He said, "No, not really." Everybody knows that minor arrests are at an officer's discretion; a 50-percent chance of walking is better than none at all. He continued:

> Sometimes when I know a guy is 10-30 [wanted], I like to say, "Pick a number between one and ten."
> He'll say, "Six!"
> And I'll say, "Put your hands behind your back."
> "That ain't fair, man!"
> But you gotta have fun.

Heroin addicts (except when they are going through withdrawal) are notoriously docile and nonconfrontational, facilitating easy arrest. Low-level drug dealers also serve as easy targets for loitering violations, as these dealers must remain near their drug stash. Although being a drug addict is not an arrestable offense, drug addicts are easy targets for arrest while they hustle for money, search for their next hit, or possess small amounts of drugs. Arrests are by definition "hands-on" and demand close physical contact. Junkies often stink and carry communicable diseases, but unlike people high on other drugs, they never fight. While police officers would like suspects to be docile, noncontagious, and sweet smelling, they'll settle for one out of three. Handcuffing and searching a suspect is physically intimate and often unpleasant for both parties involved. But it is certainly better to arrest than to be arrested.

Arresting a suspect for a minor crime is often easier than articulating the "reasonable suspicion" to stop a suspect for a more serious crime.[3] An anonymous call for drug dealing does not give an officer much additional legal authority vis-à-vis the suspect. Anonymous calls are a tricky legal area. Most calls come in anonymously and most anonymous calls are not legitimate. Yet police cannot ignore any call for service. If an anonymous call comes for an armed person, police will search the suspect, knowing that any case probably would not hold up in court. Police concern themselves with their safety, taking a gun off the street, making an arrest, and perhaps preventing a homicide. But if anonymous calls did give police the right to search, some police officers would be quick to call 911 whenever they needed to search a suspect.

Without reasonable suspicion, a police officer's power is limited to requesting that the person in question move elsewhere or consent to a search. It is far easier and defensible in court to arrest a suspect for a minor violation, then search the suspect "incident to arrest" (though an "arrest incident to a search" is not unheard of). The "probable cause" needed to arrest a suspect—for a minor crime of trespassing, open container, littering, failure to obey a lawful order—is much easier to articulate than the "probable cause" needed to search a suspect.

A group of low-level drug dealers sits under a no trespassing sign on the stoop of a vacant building and is ordered to go home, "Or I'll lock you up!" Yet police can't legally order adults to go home. It is, after all, a free country. Police don't want every little request to turn into confrontation. Orders need to be followed. In order to have such authority, police need to be respected or feared. Yet if the group remains on or returns to the same stoop, the officer is challenged and forced to follow up on that threat. Most officers won't physically threaten because they don't want to be in a position, if challenged, where they have to beat somebody to live up to their word. If you promise to lock somebody up, you have to deliver, even if there's no probable cause for a drug lockup.

More detailed arrest threats are more credible. "Move or I'll lock you up" is too vague. Better is: "It's 2:30 right now. I'm going to get a cup of coffee. I'm going to come back at 3 AM. You've got a half hour to disappear. If I see you on the street after 3 o'clock, you'd better put on a sweater because it's cold in Central Booking."

Officers who do not want to make an arrest will be careful not to threaten people with arrest or do so only at the end of their shift, when they know they really won't see them again. Wanting a lockup, officers will pick the unlucky or rude one from the group and place him under arrest. "I'm locking you up," an officer may say, " 'cause you didn't listen to me. I told you to go home or I'd lock you up. You didn't. So I did. Maybe next time you'll do what I say." The trespassing arrest is legal, but police want the suspect to believe that the real crime is failure to obey rather than the technical violation of sitting on a stoop in front of a "no trespassing" sign. And though probable cause for a search for drugs was lacking before the arrest, drugs can be found in the search incident to arrest, turning a bullshit lockup into a good arrest.

A nonviolent domestic dispute serves as another example of using the law to gain extralegal authority. A woman calls police because she is sick of her baby's father coming home and being rowdy after a night of drinking. An officer wants the drunken man to spend the night elsewhere. The girl-friend is not afraid of the man. Though the officer believes this argument will continue and perhaps turn violent, there is no cause for arrest. Police may not order a person from his or her home. But an officer can request to talk to the man outside his house. At this point the officer might say, "If you don't take a walk, I'm going to lock you up." The man, though within his rights to quietly reenter his house and say goodnight to the police, is more likely to obey the officer's request or engage the police in a loud and drunken late-night debate. The man may protest loudly that the offi-cer has no reason to lock him up. If a crowd gathers or lights in neighboring buildings turn on, he may be arrested for disorderly conduct.

When an officer decides to make an arrest, he or she has determined that probable cause exists. While a person with good demeanor can avoid arrest in many circumstances, once handcuffs are on a suspect, there is almost no chance to "talk your way out of an arrest." An officer is often asked, "What am I being locked up for?" The common response is, "You'll read it on the charging documents." Officers will not debate legal theory on the street. Once the cuffs are on, there's usually very little to say.

Citizens in the Eastern District—African Americans— are routinely and legally asked by police if they have iden-tification. This rarely happens in better-off neighborhoods. Though there is no obligation to respond, police officers may always ask people their name, where they are going, and where they live. Failure to carry ID or go by one's legal name is nearly universal among those questioned by police in the Eastern District. Rapper Ice-T explained both sides of this phenomenon in his 1988 rap, "Drama":

> Police: What's your date of birth? What's your real name?
>
> Ice-T: I stuck to my alias, I know the game. If they don't know who you are, then they don't know what you've done.
>
> Police: You're just makin' this harder on yourself, son!

The flaw in the street's code is that without identification, all offenses, even nonarrestable offenses, become arrestable (unless, of course, you're actually wanted for arrest. In that case not carrying ID does make a lot of sense). You can't write a ticket to a person who can't prove their identity. Through this power of arrest, police gain the leverage needed to control a suspect's behavior. Most drug suspects partake in multiple, if minor, illegal activities. Street-level drug dealers are, more often than not, rowdy teenagers who drink, shout, litter, and curse.

The discretionary enforcement of minor offenses is the main tool by which police officers arrest a large number of drug suspects. These discretionary arrests are neither the blind enforcement of "zero-tolerance" nor some more enlightened problem-solving strategy. Rather, police officers use arrest to establish the authority necessary for the voluntary compliance of future orders, particularly extralegal orders that cannot be backed with arrest.

Once an officer has probable cause for arrest—and a smart officer tries to have legitimate probable cause for *something*—then any disobeyed command or bad attitude can result in arrest. Officers gain compliance from a suspect and control of a situation by implying that arrest decision is based entirely on personal—even extralegal—discretion rather than the more mundane, legitimate, but extremely minor or technical violation of the law. Commands are expressed in specific personal terms for which there can be no acceptable rejoinder.

On street corners in Baltimore's Eastern District, people—usually young black males involved with drugs—are arrested when they refuse to obey a police officer's orders to move or talk back to police. This should come as no surprise when one thinks of the lessons of police training: follow orders and respect authority. On the street this approach works with decidedly mixed results.

Responding to a report of broken glass at 6 AM, two guilty kids were found on the corner. One officer walked one of them home. Another officer made the other kid, maybe twelve or fourteen years old, recite the alphabet backward. He then "gigged" the bottle breaker push-ups for each mistake. The child went through a whole academy workout of push-ups, jumping jacks, and leg lifts. Two people sat on the stoop across the street. I saw in their faces that they approved. The first officer came back and talked to the stoop sitters. He then whispered to me, "When you see people watching this shit, it's best to talk to them just to make sure. Make sure they're on your side." Ironically though this resolution wasn't by the book, push-ups *are* what we learned in the police academy.

Collars for Dollars

Though just 7 percent of Baltimore City lives in the Eastern District, the district accounts for almost a quarter of
the city's roughly 100,000 annual arrests. This is not part
of some greater crime-prevention strategy. Nor are these
arrests spread evenly throughout the department. Some
specialized units basically specialize in arrests. Even within
individual patrol squads, a few officers make the majority of
the arrests. Officers who want arrests make a lot of them.
Officers who don't, won't. Within reason, and for good reason, in high-arrests areas, most arrests are at the discretion
of the individual police officer. For the department, arrests
are a way to quantify police productivity and efficiency.
These are your tax dollars at work. If the homicide numbers
aren't going down, at least arrests show that police officers
are doing *something*. For police officers, discretionary arrests are a way to make a buck.

While "collars for dollars" is more a New York term,
the concept of arresting people for profit exists in Baltimore as it does in all police departments. Each prosecuted
arrest requires multiple court appearances by the police
officer as there are always numerous postponements. For
officers who want overtime money, court is an easy way to
get it. More serious cases can drag on over many months,
even years—that's a lot of overtime. When not on scheduled duty, Baltimore police officers are paid time-and-
a-half overtime and guaranteed a minimum of two-hours
pay for each court appearance. With the exception of
traffic court, police officer testimony is rarely required,

perhaps in about 5 percent of all cases. Leaving aside traffic court, I testified twice in about a hundred paid court appearances. None of my cases went to a jury trial. Yet an officer's presence is required even when no testimony is needed. An officer who is working a shift will be summonsed to court only when needed. When off-duty, however, police officers must come to and will be paid for all court appearances.

One advantage to working the midnight shift is that 9 AM court is soon after the 8:12 AM end of shift. If a case is not prosecuted, officers can punch in at 9 AM and punch out at 9:01 AM, a practice known as the "9:01 Club." This is considered the ideal arrest to maximize overtime pay and minimize time in court. Active officers with a court appearance per day can add 30 percent to their take-home pay, a huge incentive to some. "Court is like our heroin," one officer explained, "It's just something we need!" While police officer pay is lower in Baltimore City than most other jurisdictions, paychecks in Baltimore City can be larger: "You might get paid more in the [Baltimore] County. But you can make more here [in the city]."

Most officers want overtime, but for some, myself included, the hassles of court outweighed the pay. For one officer, it was the lengthy commute during off-hours: "Fuck no, I don't want court. Like I want to come here on my day off. Two hours [pay] ain't worth it. With my drive, I'm going to spend more on gas. Or what if you get 1:30 [PM] court? I'm supposed to work midnight to eight, drive home, sleep for three hours, drive to court, sit around for a few hours, have the case be postponed, and then go back to work that night? No thank you. I used to make more arrests, and then they started banging us for no-shows [punishing officers for failing to appear in court]. Fuck it."

Most courts are open regular business hours. Police schedules are not. Court time is scheduled without consideration for an officer's work and sleep schedule. An officer on the midnight shift may receive an afternoon summons while an officer in a specialized unit working 7 PM to 3 AM will be expected to appear in court daily at 9 AM. As police do not work Monday to Friday, court cases are often in the middle of officers' weekend. There is no "officers' lounge" in court. Nor coffee. Nor may one read in the courtroom to pass the time.

Knowing an officer must be present for a case to proceed, some suspects use postponements strategically. Other suspects simply don't have their act together. The first postponement is usually because the suspect does not have representation. The second postponement often comes when the suspect failed to secure or meet with their court-appointed attorney. And then, of course, postponements happen for various legal reasons.

Booking

Arrests are labor intensive and time consuming. After an arrest, the officer must complete the booking process before going home. This can easily become overtime. The simplest arrest, something like loitering, takes about an hour for the arresting officer to process: paperwork relating to the arrest, paperwork relating to the charging of the prisoner, and a commute to Central Booking for court paperwork. In most districts, but not in the Eastern District, police could save time by completing the charging papers on a computer at their district. Our computers were always down. It was never clear whether this was a technical glitch or a means for the state's attorney office to question our reports in person.

The amount of time needed to process an arrest can vary greatly: computers go down; shifts change; juveniles are booked separately from adults; prisoners demand medical attention (officers try very hard to avoid a multihour trip to Johns Hopkins Hospital—being under arrest does not allow you jump the hospital's waiting-room queue); property and evidence must be submitted; drugs must be photographed and submitted; and wagons must be available for prisoners' transport. Given these uncontrollable variables, officers are very hesitant to make arrests or get in situations likely to lead to an arrest toward the end of their work shift.

To control overtime pay, superiors also discourage late discretionary arrests. While a legitimate late arrest may result in a few extra hours of overtime pay, the sergeant signing the overtime slip is likely to ask details about the arrest to confirm the legitimacy before adding an extra hour or two and giving very explicit instructions to "go straight home." Officers abusing squad overtime could quickly find themselves detailed to foot patrol as punishment. When officers want overtime, they go to court.

The following is a timeline for a particularly lengthy arrest for a drug offense involving the arrest of two suspects, one adult and one juvenile. To complete the paperwork and booking process more than eight hours were needed. Though the details are specific to one case (described in greater detail on pages 132–34), both drug arrests and juvenile arrests are time-consuming. Given the circumstances, the time needed for this case was not extraordinary. The volume, variety, and redundancy of paperwork in the police department is, to the uninitiated, shocking:

1:15 AM   Receive description of drug dealing.

1:30 AM   Arrest suspects.

1:45 AM   Wagons come. Adult is transported to jail. Juvenile is transported to the Eastern District police station.

2:00 AM   Give very stern lecture to family.

2:10 AM   Go to Eastern District. Two officers complete the paperwork.

4:45 AM   District paperwork completed. Transport juvenile to Northern District (where juveniles are booked). Booking at the Northern District can take anywhere from one to four hours. On this occasion, there is no wait and everybody is working quickly.

5:30 AM   Return to the Eastern District via the gas pumps to put air in one of the tires. The tire has had slow leak for a day or two, but the previous shift said that there is no spare tire available. Back in the Eastern District, I prepare the drugs for submission. I watch twenty minutes of *The Simpsons* at the front desk and eat lunch.

6:15 AM   Arrive at downtown headquarters to submit drugs. I hear a hiss from the car's tire.

7:00 AM   Leave Headquarters. I don't want the car to be stranded in the Central Booking facility with a flat tire. I return the car to the Eastern District and take an available jeep.

7:30 AM   Leave Eastern District for Central Booking.

7:45 AM   Arrive at Central Booking.

7:55 AM   Computers at Central Booking go down.

8:12 AM   End of midnight shift. Computers working again.

8:30 AM   Finish Statement of Probable Cause. Discuss case with assistant state's attorneys at Central Booking.

9:00 AM   Leave Central Booking. Transport an officer who was working the 4 PM-to-midnight from the previous day to the Southeast District.

9:30 AM   Return to Eastern District. Prepare case folder. Fill out daily personal statistics.

9:50 AM   Work completed, I leave the Eastern District and head out for a drink.

In addition to preparing the drugs for submission (photographing the drugs in a heat-sealed bag and filling out an arrest log and a drug book), twenty-one forms and labels, nineteen of them in longhand, were completed in five different locations: one primary incident report, one supplement report for the incident, one arrest form, one statement of probable cause, one charging document for the adult, one juvenile custody form, one juvenile supplement listing the charges against the juvenile, one list of prior arrests for the juvenile, two seized property forms, five property submission forms, one lab request for drug analysis, one pink property tag for a property bag, two envelopes for property submission, and two envelopes for money submission.

While booking a prisoner or submitting evidence, officers are out of service and cannot answer calls. On the midnight shift, officers usually wait until the evening slows down before booking prisoners. On day shifts, officers must leave their posts effectively unpoliced while their squadmates reluctantly pick up calls and paperwork. Being out of service too much, particularly during busy times, is discouraged by those who must cover for the arresting officer. One night, two officers were trying to remain out of service in order to conduct surveillance of a drug corner from the second floor of a vacant building. Another officer disapproved, saying:

> It pisses me off when people go on covert and then don't handle their calls. It's one thing if someone else handles the CDS or loud music, but if it's domestic or burglary or something you have to write on, you've got to take that call. . . . The number one priority of patrol is to answer calls. I don't want to have to handle someone else's call so they can make an arrest. . . . If you want to do drugs, then go to the drug squad. But if you're going to be on patrol, then you've got to pick up your calls. We don't have time for all that other shit. It's not fair to the rest of us to handle your calls because you're trying to get some big lockup.

Another officer said:

> I think there are two kinds of humps [lazy officers]: one is someone who doesn't answer calls on their post and tries to stay out of service, the other is someone who doesn't make a lot of arrests. I may not lock a lot of people up, but I think someone is humping out when they make bullshit lockups and I have to answer calls on their post.

Given the amount of time an arresting officer may be out of service, superiors occasionally discourage arrests. Many officers called in sick one day and there weren't enough officers to cover all the posts. At roll call the shift commander said: "Use discretion. I only want felony arrests or if you have to, like domestic violence. Tell the knucklehead on the corner to go home. You can get him tomorrow. We've got a good dispatcher, Larry, who can get through the calls." An officer later complained, "I don't mind of they're really sick, but if they're just slick. . . ."

Judge Dread: Problems in Prosecution

Unlike detectives, who arrest a suspect after a lengthy investigation, patrol officers typically arrest suspects at the scene of a crime. For patrol officers, there is rarely any doubt as to a suspect's guilt: a man is found with drugs or a kid with a bloody knife is standing near a cut friend. Within a few hours of an arrest, the arresting officer submits a "statement of probable cause" to a representative from the state's attorney's office. The probable cause needed for an arrest is much lower than the judicial standard of "guilty beyond a reasonable doubt." The gap between probable cause and beyond a reasonable doubt is the root of much conflict between police and the courts. The disparity between arrests and prosecution is worrisome to many. But given the differing constitutional standards of "probable cause" and "beyond a reasonable doubt," it is inevitable.

In Baltimore, the state's attorney is elected and serves independent of the mayor and the police department. While police are interested in arresting criminals, the Office of the State's Attorney wants to prosecute winnable cases and reduce their case load. The overwhelmed representatives of the state's attorney's office may refuse to press charges at their discretion. Some cases are doomed by poorly written police reports. Many more cases are thwarted by reluctant witnesses. Unlike most criminal cases, drug crimes usually have no "victim" willing to testify. These cases are usually plea-bargained: suspects are offered "time served" and probation for admission of drug possession.

Baltimore City prosecutors decline to file charges in about 15 percent of all arrests and immediately reduce the charges in another 10 percent of cases.[4] Thirty percent of minor charges are dropped.[5] Prosecutors declined to prosecute 75 percent of the 72,200 cases brought in the city's District Court.[6] In contrast, prosecutors in surrounding Baltimore County declined to prosecute 44 percent of their 20,500 cases.[7]

Police blame much of their failure of drug prohibition on the Office of the State's Attorney. One cop expressed general frustration: "We lock them up. And then they get right back out. We're doing our job. What else can we do? These guys got a record a mile long. There's nothing we can do but chain 'em up." The bumper sticker on one Eastern District officer's personal car says, "Welfare should be as hard to get as a drug conviction." Three examples illustrate officers' frustration.

One police described her observations of a drug corner: "I saw a [white] suspect slow his car down [in an African American neighborhood]. Somebody approached the car. After a brief moment I saw a hand-to-hand [drug] transaction." When the car pulled away, the officer stopped the car and told the driver what she saw. The driver consented to a search and the drugs were found. The man was arrested.

The liaison for the state's attorney invalidated the arrest, stating that the officer did not have reasonable suspicion to stop the car. The officer explained that she saw a drug transaction on a drug corner. The liaison asked the officer, "How do you know it was drugs? How do you know it wasn't an Oreo cookie?" The officer, disgusted at the events, told me, "They sit here in C.B.I.F. [the state's attorney's court liaison office at Central Booking] and tell me I don't know a drug transaction!? I'm sitting out there watching this damn things for hours and make a good lockup. An Oreo cookie!? If only it were. Then at least I'd get something out of this. I could eat the damn cookie! As it is now, I've still got these damn drugs to submit."

One particular alley had the attention of my squad. The mayor had previously declared an adjacent street corner one of the city's drug "hot spots" and promised to end drug activity on that corner. Though the mayor's worthy promise had no direct effect on our activity, we did respond to numerous citizen complaints about drug dealing. On this night, drug buyers were observed every few minutes going into the alley and exiting a few seconds later.

One police officer had borrowed a standard Radio Shack walkie-talkie set from his children. This allowed us to listen to the conversations of numerous drug dealers in the sector. The drug dealers were communicating via walkie-talkies with a lookout on the second floor of a corner building. The lookout prevented us from catching the dealers in the act of hitting off their customers. If we approached the alley, the dealers would run and scatter through dangerous vacant buildings. Instead, we focused on disrupting the trade by arresting customers. One night a taxi stopped in front of the alley. A passenger got out of the taxi, entered the alley, and then returned to the taxi about twenty seconds later. My police report stated:

On 15 Nov [20]00 at approximately 0155 [1:55 AM] Ofc Magee and Sgt Bolden observed an individual, later identified as Mr. Hicks, in the alley of 800 N Madeira (even side). This area and this alley in particular are known as a high drug area and receive numerous complaints regarding drug sales in the alley. Mr. Hicks then entered a waiting taxi (#42 Pulaski Sedan Cab, MD Tag: 013447B) on Ashland Ave. Believing Mr. Hicks to be engaged in an illegal CDS transaction in the alley, the taxi was stopped in the 700 blk of N Patterson Park by Ofc Magee and Sgt Bolden. When approaching the vehicle, this officer [Moskos] and Ofc Magee and Ofc Kuczynski and Sgt Bolden observed Mr. Hicks place an object with his left hand into the rear area of the car behind his seat. 3 blue-topped vials were found in plain view, where it was observed that Mr. Hicks placed an object. Mr. Hicks was placed under arrest. One additional vial and one gel cap were found on the seat where Mr. Hicks had been sitting (passenger side rear).

The passenger was arrested and the taxi driver, pleading innocence, was let go. The state's attorney's office nullified the arrest, stating that there was no reasonable suspicion of criminal activity, thus making the stop illegal. Officer Kuczynski said, "That's great, half the squad is out there trying to do 'real' police work and the [court] liaison says, 'Fuck you!' It's shit like this why officers start writing, 'Once upon a time . . .'" Five days later, over a beer after work, the sergeant was still upset: "All you need is reasonable suspicion to stop a man! I'm going to start documenting these cases and take it to the major. The problem with the judges and state's attorneys is that they don't live in these neighborhoods. Let a judge's wife get raped and see if they let a rapist go free!"

In a location near the previous example, I made another drug arrest. From my Statement of Probable Cause:

> On May 21, 2001 at 1 AM, block watcher #238102 called my sergeant at the Eastern District police station and reported that there was a black female and a black male selling drugs in the 2300 block of Ashland Ave. The block watcher described the female as 17–18 years old wearing a white sleeveless shirt and a blue denim skirt. The black male was described as heavyset and sitting on the steps of 2317 Ashland Ave. The caller further stated the male was taking money from drug buyers and sending the buyers to the female, who handed the drugs to the buyers from a black bag she was carrying on her shoulders. [This description was noteworthy for both its atypical thoroughness and accuracy.]

> The 2300 block of Ashland is a known open-air drug market with dozens of calls for drug violations in the previous months. From personal experience I know 2315 Ashland Ave as the source of numerous complaints from neighbors regarding drugs and disorder.

I drove by the location and observed two individuals sitting next to each other on the stoop of 2315 Ashland Ave [which adjoins the stoop of 2317 Ashland Ave] who matched the description perfectly. I drove by the location and remained one block away and in sight until backup arrived about one or two minutes later.

I stopped my marked patrol car in front of 2315 Ashland Ave and observed the female, later identified as Ms. Foster, place the black bag behind the partially open front door. While sitting on the top of the stoop, she manipulated the bag, now just out of my sight, for approximately 5 seconds.

I exited the vehicle [holding my nightstick] and approached the two on the stoop. [I wished to gain access to the bag behind the door.] I asked them, "Do you live here?" The woman stated that she did. I then gestured at the stoop in front of 2317 Ashland Ave and asked, "Would you mind having a seat over there?" The male, later identified as Mr. Taylor, got up and sat on the stoop at 2317 Ashland.

I then asked Ms. Foster, "Would you mind also having a seat over there?" Ms. Foster got up and made an attempt to close the door. [With my body] I prevented her from closing the door. At this point Ms. Foster opened the door and tried to run inside.

Ms. Foster was restrained [as she opened the door and ran through, I basically fell on her and grabbed her] at which point I saw drugs and money in and immediately (within 6 inches) around the black bag [as we wrestled, she knocked over the black bag and drugs and money came spilling out], which was behind the front door where I had observed Ms. Foster place the bag.

[Meanwhile, the commotion woke up both Ms. Foster's brother and her severely asthmatic mother, who was sleeping topless on the living room couch. The half-naked mother started running at me, rasping for breath. The brother was more hesitant. With my nightstick in hand, I told both of them to stay back while I pushed the fighting Ms. Foster out the front door toward my backup. My partner restrained Ms. Foster while I stayed inside, keeping the family at bay while maintaining control of the drugs and money as evidence. I assumed the family was interested equally in the protection of Ms. Foster and the destruction of the evidence. All the while, Mr. Taylor on the stoop, holding no drugs, believed himself immune from arrest. He never moved from his seat. Had he wished, he could have simply walked away or joined the fray, turning the tide against us.]

Based on the information received from a reliable source, my personal observation, the known drug dealing in the area, and the quantity of CDS and U.S. currency which is consistent with dealing drugs, Ms. Foster and Mr. Taylor were placed under arrest and transported to Northern [District juvenile booking] and C.B.I.F. [Central Booking and Intake Facility] respectively.

Seized and submitted were $43, 11 gel caps of heroin, and 20 clear-top vials of cocaine in and around Ms. Foster's bag. On her person was $24. Mr. Foster had $306 on his person.

The liaison for the state's attorney immediately dropped all charges against Mr. Taylor. Ms. Foster, a day shy of her sixteenth birthday, reentered the juvenile justice system. Had the source been a routine 911 call and not a more reputable "block watcher," the assistant state's attorney told me all charges would have been dropped against Ms. Foster as well. There was a good chance the block watcher would see the same couple sitting on the same stoop the following night.

While a better funded and more aggressive Baltimore state's attorney would help police and residents, ultimately, however, the roots of the problems are elsewhere. Given our constitutional liberties, specifically the Fourth and Sixth Amendments, the drug problem will not be won through arrest and prosecution. As a side note, if drug suspects were organized, they could easily end the war on drugs. If those arrested simply refused plea bargains en masse and insisted on their constitutional right to a jury trial, the war on drugs would grind to an inglorious halt in a few months as the courts and jails would seize up, unable to handle the load.

It is asked why blacks are sentenced more severely for drug possession than whites. Given relatively similar levels of drug use among whites and blacks, it is beyond doubt that African Americans suffer disproportionately from drug arrests and convictions. Discriminatory and mandatory crack cocaine laws certainly play a large role. But in truth, for the same crime, city residents (more likely to black) are often sentenced *less severely* for drug possession than suburbanites (who are more likely to be white).

Overwhelmed Baltimore City courts are much more lenient toward drug offenders than are the courts of Maryland's other counties. At the level of state's attorney, personal drug use in Baltimore is effectively decriminalized. The greatest disparity in our court system occurs not *within* any given courtroom, but *between* different courtrooms. Local jurisdictions have tremendous discretion in our judicial system. The quality of our courts—like schools, police, and fire protection—reflect local funding. They vary according to the wealth and priorities of local governments.

The perception to the contrary may result from urban drug dealers being convicted for possession rather than intent to sell. Intent is tough to prove while possession, if one is caught possessing, is equally hard to disprove. Eager to win a quick felony conviction and take a drug dealer off the street, the state's attorney's office offers a plea: reduced charges and a lighter sentence for admission of guilt. A similar drug dealer in a wealthier court district is more likely to be prosecuted for the true crime: possession with intent to sell. As policy, users arrested in the city—regardless of race, but by and large African American—will not receive jail time for drug possession. The urban drug user is usually offered a sentence of "probation before judgment" and, if lucky, offered drug treatment. Unlike city residents, suburban and rural residents, if unlucky enough to get caught repeatedly, *can* receive jail time for drug possession. When the suburban drug user and the urban drug dealer meet in jail, they may be there for different crimes despite being convicted for the same "nonviolent drug offense."

Urban Cowboy: High-Arrest Officers

Motivated primarily by a desire for court overtime pay, police officers want arrests on their own terms, ideally without

victims, complaints, or unnecessary paperwork. Young officers make more arrests than veteran officers. These officers
believe that making arrests *is* police work. In my squad, the
top three officers in arrest totals were three officers with the
least experience. An arrest-based police culture can exist in
a low-drug environment, but without a limitless supply of
arrestable criminal offenders, an arrest-based culture cannot make a lot of arrests. Neighborhoods without public
drug dealings will not produce a high number of arrests.

Arrests aren't just a patrol function. Specialized units,
like the narcotic squad, make a lot of arrests. Since these
units don't answer calls for service, they justify their exis-
tence with the quantifiable "stats" of arrests and houses
searched. Specialized units are a promotion from patrol (virtually everything is considered a promotion from patrol).
These units are not always easy to get into. In some ways
they are invitation only. But specialized units are also self-
selective. Only some officers want to be on the narcotic
squad, usually young, aggressive, high-arrest officers. Other
officers avoid such units because the work is more dangerous, hours more irregular, court more common, and tactics
and ethics more questionable.

Criminal behavior and a bad demeanor will certainly increase the likelihood of arrest. Polite people can often avoid
arrest while rude folks can talk their way into handcuffs. But
among different officers in the same squad, arrest numbers
vary wildly. If suspect-based variables—race, demeanor, even
low-level criminal behavior—were the key factors determining arrest, one would expect similar arrest statistics for all patrol officers working in the same squad policing the same
people in the same area under the same sergeant. A small pro-
portion of police make the majority of arrests. In my police

Table 6.1
Arrests per Officer (Variations between officers, six month period)

Officer	Arrests (total)	Felony arrests	Non-Felony Arrests	Traffic citations
Jake Atz	77	5	72	135
Charlie Bricknell	66	1	65	65
Terry Cox	49	6	43	59
Pat Duncan	31	11	20	18
Art Ewoldt	24	2	22	28
Gene Ford	20	8	12	20
Ross Grimsley	20	2	18	64
Tom Hamilton	18	0	18	19
Charlie Irwin	16	4	12	60
Gerry Janeski	11	3	8	40
Burt Kuczynski	10	2	8	36
Phil Lowe	10	1	9	28
Sherry Magee	4	2	2	5
Total	356	47	309	577
Mean	27.4	3.6	23.8	44.2
Median	20	2	18	36
Std Dev	22.7	3.2	22.3	34.0

TABLE 6.1 (*continued*)

Correlation Between:	F	Sig
Nonfelony arrests and felony arrests	.075	.81
Nonfelony arrests and traffic citations	.785	.001*
Felony arrests and traffic citations	.018	.95

Source: Baltimore Police Department Monthly Performance Sheets, compiled by author.

squad (see table 6.1), the three highest-arrest officers were responsible for 54 percent of the squad's total arrests. The three lowest-arrest officers were responsible for just 7 percent of the squad's total arrests. Among individual officers, there is a strong correlation between two measures of high-discretion activities: nonfelony arrests and traffic citations. Officers who make a lot of discretionary arrests also write a lot of discretionary traffic citations. There was no correlation between felony arrests and either indicator of high-discretion activity.

Officer Charlie Bricknell made a lot of arrests. He is a short, weight-lifting young officer with an attitude both aggressive and self-effacing. Though hard-headed, Bricknell is also quick to point to his faults: "I'm dumb as a sack of rocks. I am definitely not the sharpest tack in the box. . . . I'm a poster child for ADD."

While some officers enjoy the relaxation of slower periods, Bricknell says he needs to keep moving. He explained this to me: "Look, Mr. Harvard. You always got something to read. Maybe you like that. I can't sit still. Can you imagine me reading a book? I'm lucky I can spell my name. I've never read a book. I prefer to twiddle my thumbs. I won't even pick up a magazine unless it's got pictures and even then there better be some pictures of half-naked ladies or beefy guys [muscle magazines]."

In March, after the series of low-arrest memos, Bricknell decided he was going to set the record for number of arrests in one month: "The major wants stats, I'm going to give him stats. . . . I may want to transfer somewhere else some day. I want the stats . . . and Atz [who claimed to have the record for number of arrests in a four-week work period] doesn't think I can beat him."

Bricknell decided that the easiest way to make lockups was to arrest people for violating bicycle regulations. Many bikes, at least late at night, are used by drug runners and drug lookouts. At night, all bikes are required to have a light. Bricknell would stop bicyclists for this violation. If the rider had identification, he would write a citation. Most people didn't have identification. These riders were locked up.

Bricknell defended his actions:

I lock up bicyclists. It's called zero tolerance. If you're biking in violation of the law, I'm going to write you a ticket. At 3 AM, you need a light. You ever seen a light here? If you don't got ID, C.B.I.F. All those humps [less active officers] can call me whatever they fucking want. I don't see them arresting Al fucking Capone.

It's legal. And I'm gonna do it. If they don't want to get locked up, all they gotta do is follow the law. It's even easier. All they gotta do is carry ID! But boy, do they hate me at ECU [the evidence room where the bikes were submitted as prisoners' property].

Our sergeant was supportive: "Look, I don't know what his motivations are. But I think it's good. He's locking people up, which is more than half the people in this squad. You think the lieutenant doesn't like those stats? It's good for all of us. And he gets a lot of CDS off those lockups. Most of them are dirty. And it's all legal.

Another sergeant was dismissive, "I wouldn't accept those as arrests. That's not real police."

Our sergeant responded, "But the lieutenant eats that shit up! . . . As long as the lieutenant likes them, I'm all for it."

Bricknell set the record with twenty-six arrests that month.

Other squad members were mostly dismissive of this particular high-arrest strategy. One said, "Giving tickets to people on bikes who have no money? That's just wrong." Another officer said, "It's stupid. But if that's what he wants to do with his time, good for him. I couldn't do it. But he doesn't care what people think." Another said, "Man, with Bricknell and Atz, it's like Tweedledee and Tweedledum. One's pulling over every bike, and the other is locking up every junkie that comes from the Southeast [District]. Is it making the sector any safer? I don't think so."

Officer Atz, who had more experience than Officer Bricknell, defended his own high-arrest work style: "Unless it's a busy night, I'm going to jack-up whoever I can. They [drug dealers] may not all have drugs on them. But nine times out of ten, one of them is dirty. It may not even be what they're dealing. Maybe just a blunt for "personal consumption." Either way, I win. A good lockup or 9:01 court. I don't like to sit on my ass and hump out all night. I've got a short attention span. I need to go out and do something."

I asked Atz about his predilection for loitering arrests. He replied, "Sarge really likes arrests, and I give them to him. . . . Conspiracy to possess. Loitering. I don't give a shit if they [state's attorney representatives] won't take it. That's their problem." The sergeant defended Atz's high-arrest strategy as well: "Crime right now is all on Twenty-Two and Twenty-Three Post. And if you start knocking off [arresting] one or two [addicts] a night, you start making a difference. That's what we did in Twenty-One Post. It works!"

Not Getting into Nothing: Low-Arrest Officers

One rookie officer in the Western District proudly said, "If it don't come out over the radio. I don't get involved. . . . I don't mess with nobody." While such an attitude is, of course, undesirable in a police officer, from a police officer's perspective it makes perfect sense. Officers who "look for trouble" open themselves up to use of force, physical danger, and the likelihood of civilian complaints. There is very little incentive and considerable disincentive to work more than the minimum required. A police organization embroiled in accusations of misconduct or political scandal might prefer that police officers stay out of trouble rather than aggressively taking the initiative. Politicians are more afraid of one "bad" police shooting than they are of a dozen criminal shootings.

Older officers making fewer arrests can be defensive about their low arrest totals, claiming that their arrests are "quality" or that the department will punish them if a prisoner complains about treatment. But many older officers simply admit they got tired of policing cowboy-style. The quality of low-arrest officers is hard to judge and almost impossible to quantify. Ultimately patrol officers are judged by quantifiable "productivity stats." But it is very easy for police officers to get away with doing very little work. If you stay out of trouble and make the occasional arrest, nobody in the police department will give you a hard time. Some low-arrest officers are simply lazy. Others are burnt-out. A few are simply afraid. But some low-arrest officers are excellent police. These officers see arrests as a sign of failed policing that leads to disorder and crime. Peace keeping in an underappreciated role for the patrol officer; officers receive no official credit for informally defusing situations.

Officers who ride together for the first time will ask each other about their work related interests. On my first night riding with Officer Lowe (from table 6.1), he asked me, "What are you into?" But then quickly added a twist: "Whatever it is, we're not doing it. I don't get into nothing." Later that evening he explained: "I got sick of court. I don't arrest people anymore. And I don't go to court on my day off. You don't get rewarded for arrests. I prefer to sit on my post and prevent. I don't want to see [crime] pins on my map."

On another occasion, Lowe talked about his motivations and the department's emphasis on arrests and stats: "The thing about this emphasis on stats is *I* haven't changed. I've policed the same way for the past five years. I guess when I first came out I was more gung-ho, jacking people up [stopping and searching people]. But then I got shot at. It's a humbling experience. . . . Now my priority is to me. I'm going to go home to me and my family."

Once I was backing up a call for loud music. Lowe and his partner were there. A man was giving the officers a hard time, saying, "It ain't that loud!" Officer Lowe's partner yelled at the man, "Lower the music!" After some mumbling, the man went inside and the music got quieter. As we turned around to leave, the man came out defiantly and said, "I didn't even turn down the music, I just moved the speaker!" Then the man commented about the presence of three white cops.

Officer Lowe, smoking a cigarette, slowly went to the man and said sternly, "You remember when I was here before? When you were pretty cut up? I helped you out and I treated you with respect." On hearing that, the man's attitude changed completely: "Yeah, you did. I respect you. I remember you and I respect you for that." The officer asked, "So why you gotta be acting like all this now?" The man sheepishly replied, "I'm sorry. I respect you for what you did," and then quietly went inside. Lowe told me he didn't remember the details of the previous encounter. But it was a case of domestic violence that involved a broken window and the man being "cut up pretty good."

On another occasion Lowe and I were riding together at 2:30 AM Saturday morning. We came across a group of seven young people sitting on their stoop and the stoop of the vacant building next door. They were all drinking bottles of malt liquor. Music was playing from a boom box, but not very loudly. There had been no complaint dispatched. Officer Lowe asked them for ID. Surprisingly all but one had ID. Only one was over twenty-one. Lowe told them they weren't old enough to drink. He asked them to get off the vacant building's stoop and to take the beer inside. We were polite, as were the youths. When we left, Lowe said, "That's what pisses me off. I think I handled that well. I like to think that now they respect me a little more, too, because I wasn't a dick. Would I be doing a better job if I locked them up? But I don't get any credit for good policing." Six arrests (for underage drinking in public) would be an impressive month's haul for any officer, especially Officer Lowe.

On a third occasion, soon after school ended for the summer, Lowe was walking in the courtyard of a low-rise public housing complex after midnight. A group of young teenagers was shouting and playing. Lowe stopped the juveniles and asked to see their parent or guardian. When an appropriate adult was found, Lowe lectured her about the need to respect the city curfew and honor the peace of her neighbors late at night. The process took about an hour. Lowe explained his actions to me:

> Where are their parents? Who knows. Grandma acts all concerned if I'm there. But they don't give a shit. If they did, they wouldn't let their kids hang out and drink in the middle of the night. I just try and be a buzz kill so they drink somewhere else. . . . Everybody thinks I'm a hump. And maybe I am. But I like to keep things quiet. If Cox wants to run around chasing punks, that's fine. But I prefer to take a nap. [My] post is quiet. I walk foot here for a few days [after school gets out] to make sure people don't think this is where the summer party is. You see what's going on 700 Port [St.]? They can go party there. A few hours of work now will keep things nice and quiet for the rest of the summer.

Unlike younger officers, Office Lowe was resigned to remaining on midnight patrol in the Eastern. He saw no benefit is having good "stats" and claimed not to care how he was judged.

"*I Love This Bullshit!*": Morale and Arrests

While arrests are most determined by the individual officers, overall morale greatly affects police arrest discretion. While some officers rarely make any arrests, even high-arrest officers will stop "producing" during periods of low

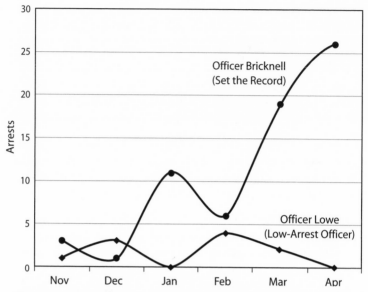

Figure 6.1. Arrests Over Time for a High-Arrest and a Low-Arrest Officer.

morale: "It's a cliché, but it's true. If you don't do nothing, you can't get in trouble. I used to go out there and bust my balls. But after you get a complaint or two, bullshit ones, you say fuck it. If this department won't defend me, assumes I'm guilty, I'm not going to do shit." Officer's arrest numbers can vary greatly over a short period of time. Figure 6.1 (above) shows the variation in monthly arrest numbers for two different officers. Officer Lowe (from table 6.1), the low-arrest officer, made ten arrests during the six-month period. His monthly arrest totals ranged from zero to four. Officer Lowe made no arrests in April while Officer Bricknell made twenty-six arrests.[8] Yet Bricknell made only three arrests in November and just one arrest in December. A few anecdotes from a period of a few months illustrate the effect of morale on officer productivity.

One officer did not come to work one day, as he had been approved for a day off. However his day off had been disapproved without his knowledge. When he returned to work he was charged with being AWOL, a fireable offence. He was angry when he told me: "I could do shit out here! Write warrants, get guns, but you see the support you get? It's not worth it. So you just answer calls. If you're out there doing your job, you're going to get complaints against. Someone will go to the phone and say, 'I was locked up and I didn't do nothing!'"

Another night, in roll call it was announced that the mayor's daughter reported that the police station's parking lot was very dirty. The memo decreed that no more trash be left in the parking lot. The shift supervisor reading the memo rolled his eyes. In typically crude humor, Officer Atz immediately asked, "Daughter? How old is she?" Somebody said ten years old. Officer Atz made a spanking gesture and said, "That's perfect! I like them young!" The shift supervisor rolled his eyes again. Atz is a decorated officer with the highest arrest totals in the squad.

In early December, a brief and official memo, universally called a "95," was required from every officer who failed to make at least one arrest in the previous four-week work period. Until then, there had been no formal pressure to make arrests or write traffic citations. As a squad, many members felt that the different work styles of various squad members complemented each other. I asked my sergeant about the real significance between my one arrest and the other officers' zero arrests. The sergeant said that the difference came from above: "If you make an arrest, I don't have to write a 95 on it. Now I have to write a 95. And they have to write a 95, too!" He explained to me: "This is Compstat bullshit. It's all numbers. The major goes downtown and gets grilled if they see a zero in any category. So now we can't put zeros down for anything. . . . If I get yelled at, then I'm going to be pissed. . . . Look at the list, you made an arrest. They didn't say anything about you. But Janeski and Irwin had no arrests. . . . There's no excuse in fifteen [work] days not to make one arrest!"[9] The sergeant told Officer Janeski, one of the officers with no arrests: "Make one freakin' arrest. It will keep them off my back and me off your back." Janeski said he was unwilling to police aggressively because he did want to be the victim of a lawsuit or internal investigation: "Sarge says some people are just coming in here to get a paycheck. But is that wrong? I don't want to lose my job and my retirement because some idiot doesn't pull over and kills a pedestrian. . . . What if I turn on my lights and he makes a right on Washington [the wrong way down a one-way street] and slams into someone on the other side of the street? Who's to say I wasn't chasing them? Me!? What's wrong with wanting to avoid lawsuits? IID [Internal Affairs] numbers? It's not worth it. I want to retire."

An officer explained the difference in arrest numbers among squad members: "Look, you can go out there and try and get into shit or you can be a hump. The more shit you do, the more lockups you'll get. But if you want lockups, you just pick up junkies. You stop cars. You can lock up as many as you want. A lot of stuff you don't have control over. Domestics? You've got mandatory arrest. If someone is cut, you cuff the dude with the knife. But those aren't usually on-view. And if they are, it's hard to run from. Anyone can make bullshit lockups. But sometimes you just get tired of it all." After the low-arrest memo criticizing officer with poor "stats," squad monthly arrest totals decreased from seventy-three to fifty.

There was a surveillance camera on Lanvale Street to which a police officer, often taken from a regular patrol post, was assigned to guard twenty-four hours a day. The irony of taking an officer off patrol to guard a camera was not lost on the unfortunate officers detailed to guard the camera. One night the officer was from another district. He said:

> I hate this unit. I got on the Lieutenant's bad side and now I'm guarding this camera for eight hours a day . . . This ain't why I became a cop . . . He said I have the lowest stats in the squad. I told him I just don't want to put my name on a lot of things. He didn't like that. A lot of these things, chasing smelly people down an alley, I don't want to be part of it. . . . [Someone] came on a ride-along once and said, "Wow, you guys really do work." We're just doing other things. I think people with a stolen bike *do* deserve police service. I think that's worth a few hours of my time.

Another officer added, "Shit, they deserve it more. They bought that bike legit with money they earned from a job."

New Year's Eve is a hair-raising night to work. Traditionally many residents celebrate by shooting guns in the air. Starting a few minutes before midnight, literally hundreds of gunshots are discharged: big guns, small guns, even a few automatics. After the very intense initial volley, frequent gunfire is heard till 1:30 AM, after which things calm down and remain relatively quiet. The sheer number of guns in the area illustrates both the need for and the futility of gun control laws.

For self-preservation, police traditionally take cover and do not patrol between midnight and 1 AM. Commissioner Edward Norris, in his first year in Baltimore, decided to police New Year's Eve aggressively. He canceled all regular and vacation days off. My sergeant promised to keep me safe and partner me with an experienced officer. My partner and I arrived early to work figuring that we could get a safer parking space in the district lot rather than on the street, were less likely to be shot on the way to work, and perhaps could relieve other officers so that they could leave before midnight.

The shift commanding lieutenant called in sick. He said he had hives. With all other officers reporting for work, there was an entirely predictable shortage of cars and radios. We scrounged up equipment from officers happy to call it a night and left the station around 11 PM. After getting coffee at Dunkin' Donuts, we drove around our post a bit before retiring to a covered place near Hopkins Hospital to ring in the New Year. As gunfire began, my partner's girlfriend kept calling, upset that he wasn't with her. My partner said to me, "She's yelling at me like it's my fault. Like I want to be on New Year's Eve rather than with her. 'Your career is always screwing you.'"

New Year's gunfire is not, in general, aimed at people. But police officers make attractive targets. Despite our attempts to lie low until the shooting stopped, some officers were on the street facing gunfire. We were willing to help other officers, even if we thought they were stupid to put themselves in harm's way. We left our protected space around fifteen minutes after midnight.

We were careful to keep moving and I kept my gun un-holstered in my lap. Between gun volleys, I asked my partner why he had stayed in the Eastern all his seven years: "I can't get out . . . I've put in for [a lot of promotions and even straight transfers]. But none came through . . . One time I solved a homicide on the day it happened. A witness said Funk-funk did it. I knew right away who that was and where he lived, Spring Street. I know this area. So I go there and get the guy and the gun. Later the Lieutenant tells me that I'm too valuable and he can't afford to have me leave midnights. So what do you get for doing good work?"

Over the radio, with gunfire crackling in the background, an officer shouts, "We're pinned down!" Later the pinned-down officer, a sergeant from another district, said that he and his partner heard shots and went down an alley. They were behind a wall when the gunfire went from in the air to toward them. The cinderblock wall they were behind was being blasted to shreds. He said, "When the bad guys paused to reload, we ran like hell."

An officer with over thirty years was upset at this behavior: "What the hell were they doing going down that alley in the first place? It was a dead end alley! They don't know the district. Why are they going places they don't know and risking death? They go down a dead end alley and get pinned." He added, "It's dumb enough to run down an alley chasing a guy with a gun. But to do so on New Year's is particularly dumb. A drunk guy is more likely to turn around a take a few pot shots."

Around 1 AM, churches let out and ladies in their church hats and men in their Sunday best walk home or to their cars, an incongruous presence amidst gunfire. The district quieted down around 1:30 AM and remained calm after that. Most years a person or two gets hit with falling bullets. Such injuries can be fatal, but usually aren't severe as the terminal velocity of a bullet coming down is much less than its muzzle velocity.

Police officers working in the Eastern District captured about a dozen guns that night. The following roll call, on New Year's Day, the lieutenant returned in high spirits and with no sign of hives. When he gave a routine injunctive to back each other up, there were coughs in the roll-call room. Later an officer expressed a common view: "Who the hell is he to tell us to back each other up? Where was he? Whatever respect I had for him went right down the drain."

A few days after New Year's, all officers with one or no arrests the previous month were again required to write a "95." This time the bar had been raised to two. Squad members were angry, even those who previously made a large number of arrests. While officers can know their squadmates and sergeant very well, in the chain of command there should be little interaction with the shift commanding lieutenant or district's commanding major. One officer told me, "You asked in the beginning what is it that gives everyone a bad attitude. Well, now you see. . . . How dare the major or L.T. [Lieutenant] call my work unsatisfactory when they have no idea what kind of job I do!"

I had made one arrest so was required to write a 95. My sergeant dictated a typical bullshit letter I could write, explaining my detail days off patrol and promising how I would do better next month. He also said, "Don't use the word 'omnipresence.' That doesn't fly." I wanted to write a real memo, since I planned to quit in a few months and return to school. I figured I could take one for the team. Two officers urged me to use the words "arrest quota" in the text because no police administration can admit having an arrest quota. I wrote a letter and showed it around. One officer said, "I didn't know you had the balls to write something like that! I'm surprised." Another said, "It was nice working with you." My sergeant tried to talk me out of it, but I said I didn't care what they did to me, as long as it wouldn't come back on him. Once he read my letter, he even suggested that I add the last paragraph but noted, "You didn't hear that from me!"

DATE: 7 JAN 00
ASSIGNMENT: Eastern District
To: Major Damon Rutherford
VIA: Official Channels
FROM: P/O Peter Moskos
SUBJECT: Arrest Statistics

Sir,

I respectfully report that I failed to meet the arrest quota during the last work period [28 days]. I was unaware that there was a quota and that by arresting only one person during my 12 days of patrol work [six vacation days and 10 hours of detail work] I would have to defend my policing and work ethic.

Much crime can be prevented by effective proactive policing. Additionally, many conflicts can be defused, resolved, and even prevented with such tactics as police presence, verbal warnings, and positive community interaction. These, combined with the judicial use of police discretion, result in fewer criminal acts. Arrests should not be viewed as a police goal but rather as an unfortunate necessity following the failure of police to prevent criminal action.

I believe the effectivness *[sic]* of my work can best be judged by the low level of crime on my posts during my working hours.

Nevertheless, if there is a quota, I would appreciate more clarification as to the numbers I must tally during each working period to be seen as an effective police officer.

Respectfully,
P/O Peter Moskos G556

Somewhat to my disappointment, this memo, like everybody else's, simply disappeared up the chain of command. Most likely there were filed away and held as collateral against individual officers, if ever needed.

In January, with morale lowered by the second low-arrest memos, the squad arrest total dropped from fifty to forty-six. The number of officers making no arrests increased.[10] In early February, the third and final low-arrest memo was released. It was similar to the first two:

Re: Notification of Unsatisfactory Performance

You are hereby notified that your work performance for the month of 12/31/00 to 1/27/01 is rated unsatisfactory.

Failure to make improvements in the above categories will result in an unsatisfactory rating in your 6 month performance evaluation.

Warning: Continued unsatisfactory performance can result in administrative action being taken under General Order C-2, Rule 1. Section 19.

More officers complained; the sergeant complained about officers complaining: "Those who do the most complaining are the ones doing the least work!"

One officer, whose monthly arrest total dropped from seven in December to one in January said, "They started fucking with us, so we stopped working. . . . This shit they have with the 95s? If they're going to worry about production and pressure us to make traffic stops and arrests, fuck 'em." Although squad arrests increased to sixty-one that month, three officers made zero arrests.

During this period, a memo read in roll call stated that officers in the Eastern District were using too many disposable plastic handcuffs, at a cost of seventy cents each. The irony of this memo was lost on no one. One officer said, "I love this bullshit! First they tell us to lock people up. Then they tell us we're using too many cuffs. We could just ask the whole district to march single-file down to C.B.I.F."

The vast majority of arrests do not involve sweat, struggle, or the use force. Arrests, like any action performed repeatedly, become mundane and ritualized for everybody. A typical arrest involves two or more officers asking a suspect to place his hands behind his back. This is the point at which suspects will comply, flee, or fight. The vast majority of suspects comply. Officers are quick to depersonalize most arrest situations by pointing out that they are "just doing their job." Despite what you see on shows like "Law & Order," cops rarely read Miranda rights to an arrested suspect.[11] Miranda refers specifically to a suspect being questioned while in custody. Once the handcuffs are on, question time is usually over.

Police departments seek aggressive police to work in high-crime areas. In the police world, aggressiveness is a plus. At its simplest, an aggressive officer is one willing to do more than the minimum work needed to answer calls for service. Good arrest numbers are the standard measure for an aggressive police officer. Arrests are good and more arrests are better. Young officers are the most likely to seek arrest-related action, stats, and the resultant court overtime pay. Arrests decrease when the hassles of arrests—lack of departmental support, citizen complaints, the burden of court, an ineffective court system—make putting away the bad guys no longer fun or worth the trouble. Very few patrol officers remain committed to a high-arrest style of policing after more than about five years on the force. This decrease, however, should not be mistaken for a change in an arrest-based philosophy. Most experienced officers still believe arrests are the essence of police work.

At the end of each shift, officers record their work statistics on the squad stat sheet. As in baseball, where even the weakest Texas-League single looks like a line-drive in the box score, for police, all arrests—good, bad, guilty, innocent, convicted, or never-charged—look the same on the stat sheet. The more the better. Felony arrests look like home runs. But nothing is wrong with a misdemeanor single.

For producing stats, drug violations in high-drug areas are similar to traffic violations. Police officers don't wonder *if* they can write a traffic violation, they simply have to want to find a person committing a traffic violation. Traffic citations reflect the presence of police much more than they reflect the distribution of traffic offences. Similarly, in a high-drug area, drug arrests are greatly increased by increased police presence. While much of this presence is needed to combat the violence of the drug trade, the result is police productivity, also known as arrests. An officer in a high-drug area is expected to make a few drug arrests every month. In the Eastern District, low-level arrests are quick and easy. This is intuitional, not personal. It is what I call the dilemma of race-blind policing: If police are disproportionately patrolling high-crime areas and if these high-crime areas are disproportionately minority, then even after controlling for differing levels of criminality, minorities are more likely to be stopped. Even if the system were race-blind and just, racial disparity still results from drug prohibition, drug-related violence, and increased police presence.[12]

I am not naïve enough to propose that police are race-blind. Nor am I saying that personal racism doesn't also exit. These would simply magnify the racial disparity. Sociologists spend a lot of time trying to identify various forms of hidden or institutional racism. This seems like an obvious place to start. Put very simply: increased presence will result in more people (for better and for worse) getting caught. I'm pro–police presence, but the negative effects of increased presence and mindless attempts at "zero-tolerance" policing need to be given more consideration.

CHAPTER 7

Prohibition: Al Capone's Revenge

I am like any other man. All I do is supply a demand.

—*Al Capone*

People from all social classes take drugs because drugs can make you feel better. Adults can drink at bars or smoke cigarettes at home. Some abuse legal prescription drugs. Abuse of prescription drugs is dangerous and widespread but engenders little public violence. Undoubtedly Rush Limbaugh's neighborhood remains a safe place to live because he allegedly bought his drugs inside his own home. Nobody advocates prohibition of pain killers simply because they're ripe for abuse. Those who can't afford prescriptions may self-medicate on cheaper illegal drugs. But most drug deals remain peaceful. The sale of all legal and regulated drugs is violence free. Even the sale of marijuana, by far the most popular illegal drug in the United States, generates little violence. Smokers of weed tend to buy their drugs in private from friends, colleagues, and coworkers. These transactions are, by and large, peaceful. Supply relates to demand, and everyone (or almost everyone) walks away happy.

This kind of relationship-based selling stands in marked contrast to the violence and disorder that swirl around Baltimore's open-air drug markets.[1] Crack and heroin are the drugs of choice. As addicts roam up and down the streets, children walking to school pass drug deals and discarded needles while hostile dealers shout to advertise their wares and confront residents opposed to their presence.[2] The chaos and fear in the Eastern District is the cost of illegal business. It stems from the nature of the public drug trade: issues of respect, punishment of workers, assault to collect debt, robbery of drug dealers, revenge for drug thefts, and killing to protect turf and market share.

Policymakers' reasoning, based on our experience with alcohol, is backward: Since alcohol is legal, drinkers cause trouble when they're drunk, not when they're trying to procure their drug of choice. Alcohol-related violence and drunk driving is tied directly to levels of consumption: more drinking, more death. So if public policy can control the consumption of alcohol, it can control violence. Simple—but wrong when applied to drug violence. Other drugs aren't like alcohol: Drug users aren't responsible for violence—high people just want to enjoy their high.[3] Drug violence is *business* violence. Since prohibition can't end drug dealing, dealing should be regulated and controlled. It would simply be ironic if it weren't so tragic: drug prohibition creates an unregulated, chaotic, and violent drug culture.

Maybe if we understood how we got into the fine mess we could pull ourselves out of it. Drugs became a police problem as many problems do: nobody else wanted to deal with it. Society's buck stops with the police. And prohibition prevents alternatives. American public policy has long been influenced by the deeply rooted beliefs of prohibitionists. Combined with faith in social engineering and state paternalism, the war on drugs is a morality play, a continuation of the failed temperance and prohibition movements of the nineteenth and twentieth centuries.[4]

Intemperance: Public Enemy Number One

> There is but one philosophical way of dealing with this
> liquor problem, and that is by absolute prohibition, the
> Divine way of dealing with moral evils.
> —*Prohibitionist Rev. J.A.B. Wilson, 1895*[5]

The desire to protect those perceived as unable or unwilling to resist temptation spans an oddly disjointed segment of the American political spectrum. Social "progressives" use science and logic to imposing their beliefs. Elected New York City Council members voted to ban public smoking, hydrogenated fats, foie gras, aluminum baseball bats, and even gatherings of bicycles. And these are the liberals. Conservatives talk of economics and public safety. The Religious Right sees a broader godly fight against evil.

The invocation of "evil" in the language of the nineteenth-century Temperance Movement and the twenty-first-century war on drugs is more than a trivial coincidence. To secularists, the word "evil" may be synonymous with "very bad." But to the religiously inclined, evil can represent the unified and active force of Satan in opposition to all that is good. Defining a problem as an unqualified evil makes it that much easier to draw normative boundaries and crack down on those who fall on the wrong side of the divide— the evildoers.[6] As a moral crusade, prohibition is a fight against evil, a shining path to the pearly gates. The problem with this position, both practically and theologically, is that drugs are chemicals without a moral agenda. Even drugs that are undoubtedly bad are not evil.

In America, there were attempts at alcohol prohibition even in colonial times. But modern prohibition is rooted in the Temperance and Progressive Movements of the nineteenth century.[7] Progressives—a broad-based mostly middle- and upper-class antipopulist Protestant coalition—advocated for vice laws, an eight-hour work day, prison reform, and a "good government" agenda. Their lobbies promoted parks, botanic gardens, and zoos as replacements for working-class saloons and outdoor beer gardens. The less benign Progressive agenda was rooted in beliefs of eugenics and racial superiority: immigration restrictions, racial segregation, and mandatory sterilization for the "feeble minded." Progressives felt a duty so save "their" country from the unwashed masses. That meant saving the unwashed masses from themselves.

Not all Progressives supported temperance, but the nativist middle-class Temperance Movement came to control the Progressive agenda. Politically Progressives leaned Republican while immigrants, Catholics, white Southerners, and city residents were drawn to the machine politics of the Democrats. Progressives were most influential among urban elite and in rural and wealthy small-town communities. But their battlegrounds were working-class cities where "traditional values" were most threatened. The fear was clear: "The influx of foreigners into our urban centers, many of whom have liquor habits, is a menace to good government. . . . The foreign born population is largely under the social and political control of the saloon. If the cities keep up their rapid growth they will soon have the balance of political power in the nation."[8] The solution seemed obvious: "Our nation can only be saved by turning the pure stream of country sentiment and township morals to flush out the cesspools of cities and so save civilization from pollution."[9]

Until the final passage of the Eighteenth Amendment and Prohibition, temperance supporters advocated what today would be considered harm reduction. They followed Thomas Jefferson's dictum, "No nation is drunken where wine is cheap," and promoted beer and wine as alternatives to stronger liquor. In the 1830s, after the American Temperance Union framed the argument against alcohol as a moral battle of good versus evil, they took the radical but logical step of supporting total alcohol prohibition.[10] In the early 1850s, thirteen states and many localities had adopted alcohol prohibition.[11]

As the Civil War neared its end, Progressives, having won the war against slavery, redoubled their efforts against alcohol. They portrayed saloons as destroyers of morals, families, and lives. The Prohibition Party, established in 1864, fielded its first presidential candidate in 1872. The Woman's Christian Temperance Union, established in 1874, promoted temperance education in public schools.[12] Prohibition proved most effective at limiting alcohol when enacted at a local level with popular support. Too often, however, counties and states imposed Prohibition on unwilling immigrants and cities.[13]

The Anti-Saloon League, established in 1893, brought momentum to the prohibitionists' side. The league was America's first successful nonpartisan single-issue advocacy group.[14] The Anti-Saloon League combined the moral rhetoric of personal salvation with a general hostility toward saloons. Their temperance cause addressed concrete family concerns and quality-of-life issues that resonated with many Americans. Even opponents of prohibition were quick to concede that saloons were an unsavory blend of bar, flophouse, and whorehouse. World War I's anti-German bias helped the cause by focusing public wrath on the German-American brewing industry.[15]

Supporters of prohibition promised an improved economy, crime reduction, stronger families, and sobriety. The Anti-Saloon League blamed saloons for "leading astray 60,000 girls each year into lives of immorality."[16] They estimated (in their opinion, "conservatively") that "liquor is responsible for 19 percent of the divorces, 25 percent of the poverty, 25 percent of the insanity, 37 percent of the pauperism, 45 percent of child desertion, and 50 percent of the crime in this country."[17] Led by the Anti-Saloon League's political action, thirty-one states with almost half the U.S. population were legally "dry" before the ratification of the Eighteenth Amendment.[18] But many were surprised when in last minute dealings, the Eighteenth Amendment, was broadened to include beer and wine along with hard liquor. National constitutional alcohol prohibition took effect in January 1920. The Volstead Act of Congress empowered the Department of the Treasury with enforcement responsibilities banning the manufacture, sale, and transportation of intoxicating liquors. Fifty years before the phrase was coined, the war on drugs began.

President Warren Harding optimistically predicted, "In another generation, I believe liquor will have disappeared, not merely from our politics, but from our memories." An opposing view was provided by New Jersey Governor Edward Edwards. He publicly stated a desire to keep New Jersey "as wet as the Atlantic Ocean."[19] Prohibition's opponents presciently warned of increasing federal supremacy and a dangerous new precedent: using the Constitution to restrict personal liberties rather than government authority.

During Prohibition, alcohol sellers were condemned: "Of all classes of organized criminals," said Senator Millard Tydings, "those who are engaged mainly in the manufacture, distribution and sale of intoxicating liquors constitute the greatest menace."[20] The propaganda machine of the federal government offered advice on incorporating Prohibition education into art, English, math, and social studies classes. The Bureau of Prohibition published such slogans as "The 18th Amendment stands for better boys and better business," "Obedience to law is protection," and "When we outlaw an evil we bring into being the strongest possible weapon against that evil."[21] But people didn't stop drinking.

The bulk of high-quality alcohol came over land and water from Canada. More conspicuous were "rum runners," drug smugglers usually based in the Bahamas. They waited in boats just outside the country's three-mile territorial limit and would sell alcohol to visiting boats or sprint ashore to unload. President Harding asked the Navy to intervene. Officials in the U.S. Navy refused, casting Prohibition as a domestic police issue outside their jurisdiction.[22] The U.S. attorney general sided with the Navy. In response, the Coast Guard rapidly expanded to better "protect our borders."

In the heady 1920's postwar spirit of progress and prohibition, Congress passed more drug laws: the Narcotic Drug Import and Export Act outlawed the nonmedical use of narcotics; the Jones-Miller Act established the Federal Narcotics Control Board; the manufacture of heroin was prohibited in 1924. But none of these efforts were seen as particularly effective. In 1927, an advocate for greater alcohol prohibition enforcement said, "[Alcohol prohibition] can be enforced reasonably well if proper effort is made. . . . It is already better enforced than some of our other laws as, for example, the law against narcotics."[23] The Federal Bureau of Narcotics, the forerunner of today's Drug Enforcement Agency, was established in 1930.

Better Than No Liquor at All: Alcohol Consumption during Prohibition

Some fear that ending the war on the drugs would increase drug use. The history of prohibition should lay this fear to rest. In the decade preceding national alcohol prohibition, per capita alcohol consumption declined significantly, perhaps by as much as 50 percent. Between 1919 and 1921, alcohol consumption may have dropped as much again.[24] With Prohibition, however, the government lost the ability to accurately measure and regulate alcohol production, importation, and consumption. As the debate between "wets" and "drys" was always contentious, statistics on alcohol consumption between 1920 and 1933 are notoriously unreliable. The "dry" side certainly had the home-field advantage with the moral and financial support of the federal government. At least until the Great Depression, "drys" were better organized, published more, and claimed the good words of progress, science, and even God on their side.

Clark Warburton, an economist, used the arrest rate for drunkenness in 383 cities as a proxy measure for alcohol consumption.[25] Arrests for drunkenness peaked in 1916 and decreased 63 percent by 1920. By 1928, the rate had increased to 80 percent of the 1916 level. Warburton noted, "Under Prohibition, especially during the early years, police were more strict in making arrests. . . . It is reasonable to suppose that drinking is less public and that fewer drunken persons appear on the streets relative to the quantity of liquor consumed."[26] Economists Angela Dills and

Jeffrey Miron look at arrest numbers and cirrhosis levels and propose a 10 to 20 percent reduction due to constitutional prohibition.[27]

Between 1919 and 1920, hospital admissions, alcohol-related deaths, and arrests for drunkenness all decreased. Industrialists such as Henry Ford reported increased worker productivity.[28] But Prohibition's benefits were short-lived. During Prohibition, increased grain and hops production reflected *greater* alcohol production.[29] Consumption rose throughout the 1920s. As early as 1922, alcohol consumption could easily have exceeded the 1919 level.[30] Regardless of consumption levels, total spending on alcohol increased as beer prices quadrupled and hard liquor prices doubled.[31]

Although it may seem odd that drinking increased during the 1920s, Prohibition added a certain cachet to going out and drinking. In the 1910s, intemperance was linked to backwardness, the feebleminded, immigrants of inferior genetic stock, and drunken men. Prohibition made alcohol trendy and the gave birth to the Roaring Twenties. The culture of drinking changed, probably for the better. While anybody with a bottle of gin and two glasses could open a speakeasy (and many did), the worst of the saloons were closed. Speakeasies were the first place respectable women could drink in the company of strangers. Women's drinking probably had a moderating effect on the drinking culture in general.

Alcohol remained easy to get in "wet" areas with lax enforcement. The most famous federal prohibition agent, the five-foot-tall, 225-pound Izzy Einstein, said he could get a drink in any city within thirty minutes. He and his partner, Moe Smith, were responsible for 20 percent of all Prohibition arrests in Manhattan between 1920 and 1925.[32] Will Rogers quipped, "Prohibition is better than no liquor at all" and warned, "The minute they get Prohibition they will hop on to something else[,] it will be Cigarettes . . . or something."

But Prohibition was more than speakeasies. Exemptions for religious and medicinal use were heavily exploited. The amount of liquor sold by physicians and hospitals doubled between 1923 and 1931. Medicinal alcohol production increased 400 percent.[33] Items such as raisin cakes "warned" that if placed in a jug for twenty-one days, they would "ferment and turn into wine."[34] Meanwhile bootleggers organized to meet increasing demand. Some bought entire distilleries at fire-sale prices to acquire their stock.

In 1930, the phrase "jake leg" entered the English language. Jamaican Ginger, or Jake, a small amount of ginger extract preserved in alcohol, was sold in drugstores in convenient two-ounce bottles. Jake was one of many popular "medicinal" beverages in the 1920s. Drugstores, particularly those with soda counters, proliferated during Prohibition. Jake mixed well with coffee or Coca-Cola. To evade a government crackdown on the high alcohol content of patent medicines, an adulterant thought to be nontoxic was used in the making of a large batch of Jake in Boston. In a few short weeks in March 1930, 30,000 to 100,000 people were made impotent and partially but permanently paralyzed. Their conspicuously hobbled rubber-legged walk became known as jake leg. Victims were spread throughout the East, Midwest, and South, but hardest hit were poor working-class drinkers in Kansas, Tennessee, and Mississippi.[35] Prohibitionists, like one Baptist minister in a hard hit Tennessee town, preached, "God is hanging out a red flag as a danger sign to those who violate His law."[36]

While we may think of the 1920s as a swinging era of flappers, Babe Ruth, and (ironically) alcohol, for lower-class citizens the government's war on alcohol was no joke. Edward Behr examined the *Easthampton Star* of Long Island, New York from 1920 to 1933. "No socialites, or even 'respectable' wealthy householders, were ever arraigned in the Hamptons. The victims of local Prohibition agents' zeal were invariably working-class artisans or small potato farmers, often recent immigrants with exotic Polish names."[37] New York congressman Fiorello La Guardia, who would become mayor in 1929, criticized Southern support for Prohibition as racist laws, "Only enforced among the coloured populations. . . . The white gentleman openly and freely can obtain and consume all the liquor he desires."[38] Without government regulation, moonshine and other dangerous alcohol proliferated: "There was a run on anything containing alcohol that could be used as a basis for homemade liquor—embalming fluid, antifreeze solution, solidified and rubbing alcohol, bay rum—with horrendous consequences, for, inexplicable, old rules requiring denatured alcohol to bear the POISON warning were discontinued."[39]

New brands of alcohol sprung up with names suggestive of today's drug markets: Panther Whiskey, Red Eye, Cherry Dynamite, Happy Sally, Jump Steady, Soda Pop Moon, Sugar Moon, and Yack-Yack Bourbon.[40] Deaths from poisoned liquor quadrupled from 1,064 in 1920 to 4,154 in 1925.[41] So much for the benefits of reduced consumption.

The Real McCoy[42]: Alcohol-Related Crime during Prohibition

From the creation of police in the mid-nineteenth century well into the twentieth century, the majority of police arrests in northern cities were for public drunkenness. Of those arrested, the majority were foreign-born immigrants.

In the early years of Prohibition, there was great debate about the link between alcohol and crime. Similar to the percentage of crime considered drug-related today, 50 to 80 percent of crime was estimated to be alcohol-related. Because of this, "drys" predicted that Prohibition would decrease crime from 50 to 80 percent. "Wets" noted that a majority of the nation had already gone dry in the years before national Prohibition, yet the expected reduction in crime had not materialized.

After 1920, crime rose in sync with alcohol consumption. The organized Mob existed well before the Eighteenth Amendment, but it flourished and grew with the profits from the alcohol trade. One study of thirty major U.S. cities showed a 24 percent increase in the number of crimes between 1920 and 1921.[43] "Drys" simply denied the increase in crime and blamed the media for focusing on sensational gangland killings and fear mongering.[44] But these fears were rooted in reality. Prohibition-related murders were increasing steadily.[45] Chicago had about eighty Mob killings per year during Prohibition.[46] While eighty murders a year is less than the number of prohibition-related killings today, outside of specific nineteenth-century race riots, it was a level of carnage never seen in American cities.

Federal agents killed local bootleggers, and agents were routinely indicted for homicide by local prosecutors. But the feds quickly transferred these cases to federal courts where federal prosecutors would drop the charges.[47] The government's 1931 Wickersham Commission, which opposed repeal, lowballed Prohibition's body count but still listed sixty prohibition agents and 144 civilians deaths resulting directly from law enforcement efforts.[48] "Indirect" deaths were much higher. By 1930, perhaps 1,000 civilians had been killed by local and federal agents enforcing Prohibition.[49]

By the second half of the 1920s, despite tougher laws and increased spending on law enforcement, all but the most stubborn drys conceded that crime had increased. Drys argued that Prohibition failed because it had never been effectively implemented. Prohibitionists continued to argue—both correctly and quixotically—that decreased consumption would lower crime. The solution, naturally, was greater enforcement and tougher laws. In 1927, Congress strengthened Prohibition laws. Similar to today's drug laws, New York and Michigan passed draconian mandatory sentencing laws for repeat offenders. A Michigan mother of ten was sentenced to life in prison for possession of a pint of gin.[50] Under-enforcement was also a problem: crime among bootleggers could be seen as private business and sympathetic jurors often acquitted guilty defendants.[51] Public officials were corrupted. One New York magistrate fumed, "Nine-tenths of these liquor cases are tainted with graft."[52] Prohibitionists' myopic utopian vision blinded them to these failures.

In the face of continued drinking and increased violence, Prohibition agents justified their productivity with more arrests. This clogged the courts. Over 60,000 people a year were arrested for violations of the Volstead Act.[53] While this is less than the number of drug arrests today in Baltimore alone, alcohol prohibition marked the beginning of the government's involvement in the large-scale arrest and imprisonment of nonviolent drug offenders. The federal prisons population grew dramatically.[54] In Prohibition cases, the U.S. Supreme Court allowed warrantless searches of private cars, rolled back constitutional protections against double jeopardy, and decided that telephone wiretaps did not violate Fourth and Fifth Amendment protections.[55]

In the 1920s, a loud minority of politicians spoke out against Prohibition.[56] As Prohibition's benefits failed to materialize, support for the Eighteenth Amendment decreased. While those with a fondness for drink always opposed Prohibition, many antialcohol advocates came to accept Prohibition's "cure" as worse than any drug-related disease. Repeal occurred only after *policy concerns* replaced an agenda of moral panic, public health, and godly salvation. The Great Depression and rising crime made a taxed and legally regulated drink a very popular proposition.[57] In 1932, Franklin D. Roosevelt won the presidential election on a wet Democratic platform. In 1933, the Twenty-First Amendment to the Constitution repealed the Eighteenth Amendment. Alcohol regulation returned to the state and local level. With alcohol legal, selling was regulated and homicides began an immediate and long decline. By 1938, while the economy was constricting and unemployment, despite the New Deal, was at 19 percent, the homicide rate reached pre-Prohibition levels. Not until 1974, after Richard Nixon declared a new "war on drugs" did the homicide rate top the 1933 record.

Prohibition's repeal did not bring about all the promised benefits: the economy did not improve, prisons did not empty, saloons—relabeled bars or taverns—quickly reappeared, and the Mob, rather than going quietly into the night, shifted toward prostitution, gambling, and organized labor.[58] Nevertheless, with few exceptions, the country was happy to end the Noble Experiment.[59] Prohibition was a failure. But decades of preaching against the evils of alcohol and drugs planted a prohibitionist ethos that wouldn't die.[60]

Feel No Pain: Drug Prohibition in America

Before the Eighteenth Amendment, prohibitionists pushed for a complete ban of all drugs. Early narcotic bans that permitted medicinal use were opposed by reformers as incomplete.[61] The failure of alcohol prohibition did not bring about any corresponding call for the repeal of drug prohibition. While public demand for alcohol prohibition preceded the Eighteenth Amendment, support for narcotic prohibition grew strong only *after* the implementation of national drug prohibition laws.

Heroin, an opium derivative first created in 1874, was rediscovered in 1895 by the Bayer Pharmaceutical Department and marketed in 1898 as a sedative for coughs and a nonaddictive substitute for morphine. It appeared on the illicit street market around 1909.[62] Cocaine was first isolated in the mid-nineteenth century. In the 1860s, Vin Mariani, a popular French wine fortified with both coca and caffeine, was endorsed by no less an authority than Pope Leo XIII. In 1886, during a brief period of alcohol prohibition in Fulton County, Georgia, pharmacist John Styth Pemberton created a nonalcoholic alternative to Vin Mariani. He replaced the wine with a sweet caffeine- and cocaine-laced syrup and called it Coca-Cola.[63] Until 1903, Coca-Cola probably contained about the same amount of cocaine as Vin Mariani, around six or seven milligrams per ounce. A glass of Coca-Cola might have been equivalent to a very small "line" of cocaine. For a bigger kick, stronger (and often unlabeled) concentrations of cocaine and opiates were readily available in over-the-counter patent medicines.

Heralded as a wonder drug, cocaine was considered a safe and effective anesthetic in 1884.[64] Until then, ether, nitrous oxide, and chloroform were all used as anesthetics. But their unpredictable nature made use controversial even within the medical profession. Cocaine had a year of unencumbered medicinal glory before people starting dying.[65] Over the next decade, a slow but steady stream of minor press stories described the ruin or death of doctors and chemists (and their wives) victimized by cocaine addiction.[66] Advances in anesthesiology, particularly the invention of Novocain, lessened the medicinal use of cocaine.

In 1906, Congress passed the Pure Food and Drug Act. This laid the groundwork for Federal drug prohibition by establishing the Federal Government's right to regulate the food and drug trade. While this landmark regulation did not ban narcotics per se, it effectively destroyed the sham patent medicine business by requiring accurate labeling on food and medicines.

As drug use spread from the white upper classes, society's perception of drug addicts changed. The drug addict morphed from "victim" to "fiend."[67] The victim became a criminal; and the patient, a prisoner. Until the end of the nineteenth century, fear of drug addicts and drug-related criminal behavior was by and large absent. The *New York Times* first linked cocaine to criminal behavior in 1897.[68] In 1900, the newspaper described four "morphine victims" as "human wrecks." Increasing cocaine use in the black community became an issue in the early 1900s.[69] But narcotic-related crime was still limited to minor vagrancy and the petty crime of destitute users funding their addiction.[70] As long as drug addicts are "victims," incarceration makes no sense. Early criminalization of drug use was by-and-large an attempt by localities to force drug users to enter rehabilitation programs. But as treatment was largely unsuccessful, prohibition laws remained and the responsibility for drug addiction shifted away from doctors and hospitals and toward police and prisons.

New York State—in a unanimous vote without fanfare—banned the nonmedicinal use of cocaine with the 1907 Anti-Cocaine Smith Act. The immediate result was telling: drug selling moved underground. The *New York Times* reported: "Peddlers, poor, unmoral creatures of the underworld, have sprung up to ply a thriving trade in dispensing the drug among the victims of the habit."[71] By 1908, one doctor estimated that while 80 percent of his drug-addicted patients were physicians or physicians' wives, "Few of these people are cocaine users. . . . As a rule . . . the [cocaine] habit is found confined to the lower classes of society."[72] Cocaine remained a moderately popular drug for both medicinal and recreational use. But on a per capita basis, cocaine consumption levels were probably one-fifth of today's levels.[73]

The federalization of prohibition continued. In 1914, alarmed by absurd press accounts of "one million drug-fiends," Congress banned the unprescribed distribution of opiates and cocaine with the Harrison Narcotic Act. With legitimate sellers largely out of the picture, the number of drug-related hospital admissions and deaths dramatically increased.[74] The Harrison Act may not have been the beginning of drug prohibition and the war on drugs, but it was certainly the first panicked federal response to an exaggerated drug scare.

Estimates on drug use continued to range drastically, with the higher-end exaggerations serving to further demonizing drugs. In 1915, the federal government estimated 200,000 drug users nationwide.[75] In 1919, the *New York Times* warned of 200,000 drug addicts in New York City alone.[76] But just five days later, the same paper claimed just 8,000 men between 21 and 31 addicted to drugs.[77]

The American Medical Association was a strong supporter of prescribed narcotics up to and even after the 1914 Harrison Act. But support among "respectable" doctors for legal or medicinal use of narcotics had been largely neutralized by the criminalization of drugs and unscrupulous doctors and pharmacists selling drugs. Doctor-supervised drug-treatment programs were undermined both by their limited effectiveness and a series of court decisions restricting the rights of doctors to practice drug maintenance programs.[78] At the same time, local alcohol prohibition laws—designed primarily to keep liquor away from the lower classes—may have increased the use of other drugs.[79] Likewise, the beginning of national alcohol prohibition probably increased the popularity of other illegal drugs.[80] In 1917, at least one medical doctor observed that antidrug laws increased drug use by pushing addicts away from physicians and treatment and toward the "sinuous, criminal underworld."[81]

Concurrent with the 1914 Harrison Act, New York City established the first police drug unit. "The police of this city, co-operating in a nation-wide movement inaugurated by a committee of five member of the American Medical Association, began a systematic attempt yesterday to bring into custody those addicted to the use of drugs."[82] This unit, known as the "dope squad," earned headlines of "great progress" when its officers accounted for one-third of the 1,950 people arrested citywide for possession or sale of drugs.[83] Approximately two-thirds of those arrested for drug violations had no prior criminal record.[84] In 1928, four officers in the Dope Squad were fired when an internal raid found hypodermic needles and undescribed "packages" in detectives' lockers.[85]

In the late 1920s, the Federal Bureau of Narcotics was modeled after the ineffective Bureau of Prohibition Enforcement. Many narcotic agents, including the Narcotics Bureau's first commissioner, Harry Anslinger, came directly from Prohibition units. Anslinger successfully lobbied for federal drug laws, such as the 1937 Marihuana Tax Act that effectively banned marijuana and hemp. On a practical level, drug agents did little but sieze small amounts of drugs. In 1938, federal agents confiscated 674 kilograms of opium, 558 kilograms of marijuana, 94 kilograms of heroin, 12 kilograms of morphine, and just one pound of cocaine.[86] Today *20-ton* seizures aren't unheard of, yet prices are cheaper than ever. In the 1920s, cocaine sold for about 25 cents a "grain," or $45 a gram, inflation adjusted.[87] In the 1920s, as law enforcement became more concerned with heroin, cocaine use fell out of favor.[88] Since the 1970s when cocaine remerged, the street price of cocaine in today's dollars has dropped from about $230 to $35 for a pure gram.[89]

Drug laws generally follow increased drug use by an "outside" group: cocaine became illegal after being associated with African Americans following postbellum Reconstruction.[90] Opium, associated with Chinese immigrant workers, was first restricted in California in 1875. This was perhaps the nation's first nonalcohol-related drug law. Immigrant drinkers advanced the cause of Prohibitionists.

Marijuana was legal and largely ignored until the 1910s when it became associated with crazed Mexicans in the Southwest. LSD was outlawed in 1967 after being embraced by the counterculture. Crack-cocaine laws responded to drug use among ghetto blacks.

As drug use became linked in the 1960s to social movements and the opposition to the war in Vietnam, Richard Nixon needed a wedge issue to isolate counterculture liberals. Running for president on a law-and-order ticket, he coined the phrase "war on drugs."[91] As president, Nixon followed through, outlawing amphetamines, barbiturates, and LSD. Today's system categorizing drugs based on medical use and addictive potential—nicotine and alcohol notably excepted—was created in 1969 and 1970. As drug use spread to the middle class, federal funds were set aside for drug treatment and prevention. Nixon's support for rehabilitation was strongly influenced by the fear of drug-using soldiers returning home from Vietnam as addicts. Yet, for reasons not fully understood, the vast majority of American opiate users in Vietnam were able to quit their habit when they returned to the United States.[92]

Crack, Drug Prohibition, and African Americans

Accounts of widespread cocaine use by African Americans—some sensational, some descriptive—began to appear around 1900. An oft-cited 1914 *New York Times* article described a cocaine-frenzied black man unfazed by police bullets large enough to "Kill any game in America."[93] In 1929, Drug Czar Anslinger is reported to have said, "Reefer makes darkies think they're as good as white men." While racist sensationalism seems standard in the early twentieth century, drug-related press stories seem no more racist than other stories of the era. The majority of drug-related press accounts dealt with the death of upper-class white people. Drug "victims" were rarely news unless from a prominent station in society. Drug "fiends" were usually white. Only a few stories in the mainstream press "played the race card" on drug use, and these tended to blend a patriarchal combination of sympathy, concern, and fear. Most often social problems in the African American community were simply ignored.

During the 1980s, crack cocaine changed things. Crack's murky origins in 1982 coincided with CIA fundraising for the Nicaraguan Contras and an influx of Latin American cocaine into Miami and Los Angeles. While the true story of crack may never be known, the recipe is simple: ordinary powder cocaine is heated is a solution of water and baking soda until the solids separate. The resulting mass is dried, broken into smaller "rocks," packaged, sold, and lit in a small glass pipe.

In crack's early years, many in the black community complained that not enough was being done to battle the problem. Black community leaders wanted more awareness and law enforcement. Actor and activist Ossie Davis protested, "Unless the federal, state and city governments are willing to put crack, other drugs and their attendant problems at the very top of their agendas, we are going to stay in the streets."[94] Some in the press admitted they failed to provide balanced news coverage for stories linking race, drugs, and crime.[95] Sensational and overblown accounts of "crack babies" hyped fears of a dangerous generation of black youth while real concerns about growing violence *within* the black community usually went under-reported. Congress passed strong antidrug laws in 1986 and 1988.

In a kind of "perfect storm" that brought drug dealing to the masses, crack cocaine's hold on the ghetto had many contributing factors. More cocaine was entering the United States at the same time Regan-era budget cuts made getting by, or semilegal "hustling," more difficult for many poor.[96] Before crack, cocaine dealing required financial or social capital to buy or be trusted with a costly drug. But crack is sold in single-dose units. In terms of selling and marketing, crack has more in common with "loose" cigarettes, bottles of malt liquor, and flasks of hard liquor. A crack dealer can start with ten dollars, buy a vial, and double his money with a skillful resale. Cooking and selling crack offered a new source of income for people without legitimate job qualifications. The high volume needed for low-priced sales encouraged drug dealers to conduct business in high-traffic public areas. Unlike other illegal drugs but similar to some legal pharmaceuticals, the spread of crack was at first a supply-driven marketing phenomenon.[97] In many neighborhoods, buying crack was easier and more readily available than fruit and vegetables. Poor people could dabble; many became addicted.

When crack cocaine hit the big cities, youth violence—in particular, black male handgun violence—skyrocketed. Between 1984 and 1993, the overall homicide rate for those older than twenty-four remained constant while the rate of handgun homicides among black men eighteen to twenty-four *tripled*.[98] The median age of gun-homicide offenders dropped from twenty-one in 1985 to eighteen in 1992. Killers were younger, less rational, and bad shots. The seemingly random nature of gun violence increased.[99]

Even if crack-cocaine laws and mandatory-minimum sentencing were not racist in their original intentions, the war on drugs is a de facto war against poor blacks. Outcomes that so negatively affect African Americans should place the moral burden on those who continue to advocate imprisonment as our national drug policy. Communities cannot survive when incarceration is the norm.

From 1925 to 1975, despite some variance, about 1 in 1,000 Americans was imprisoned at any given time. In 1975, there were approximately 200,000 prisoners. Thirty-two-years later, after thirty-two years of drug war, there are 2.3 million behind bars—1 in every 130 American.[100] Canada, by comparison, imprisons 1 in every 750 people. Every country in Western Europe imprisons still fewer. Pick any country and we lock up more people. America has the highest rate of incarceration in the world. This, as Eric Schlosser coined, is the prison-industrial complex:

A set of bureaucratic, political, and economic interests that encourage increased spending on imprisonment, regardless of the actual need. The prison-industrial complex is not a conspiracy, guiding the nation's criminal-justice policy behind closed doors. It is a confluence of special interests that has given prison construction in the United States a seemingly unstoppable momentum. It is composed of politicians, both liberal and conservative, who have used fear of crime to gain votes; impoverished rural areas where prisons have become a cornerstone of economic development; private companies that regard the roughly $35 billion spent each year on corrections not as a burden on American taxpayers but as a lucrative market; and government officials whose fiefdoms have expanded along with the inmate population. . . . The raw material of the prison-industrial complex is its inmates: the poor, the homeless, and the mentally ill; drug dealers, drug addicts, alcoholics, and a wide assortment of violent sociopaths.[101]

Nobody argues that prisons and prisoners are the ideal use of state and federal tax dollars, but it is not clear how the prison-industrial complex can be defeated. In 2004, California's Proposition 66 would have softening the state's "three strikes and you're out" law by restricting the second and third "strikes" to violent felonies. The primary beneficiaries would have been nonviolent drug offenders. After strong lobbying by California's correctional officers' union, the proposition was narrowly defeated. Prison guards, tough job though they do, should have no voice in sentencing policy. The prison-industrial complex should not become our Works Progress Administration. Incarceration is not an employment scheme.

As it stands, buyers and sellers of illegal drugs are simple cannon fodder for cops and prisons. Need an arrest to satisfy your sergeant? Hit a corner. "It's like shooting fish in a barrel," one officer said, "You'll never run out of people to arrest here." But in this barrel, it should be noted, almost all the fish are black. It's not that cops go out wanting to arrest *black* people. But cops who make a lot of arrests do so in black neighborhoods. It's easy when drug laws criminalize so many. When police have an almost arbitrary power of arrest over the majority of the populace, police and their moral perspective become an occupying force at odds with the community. This is why those most in need of police services—those most victimized by drugs and violent

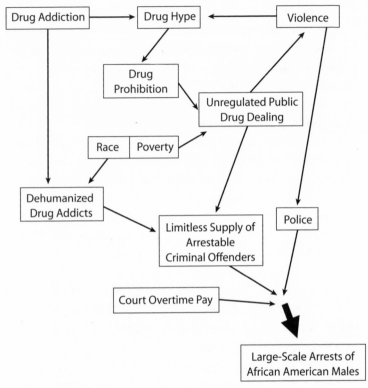

Figure 7.1. Prohibition, Public Drug Dealing, and the Large-Scale Arrests of African American Males.

crime—are most likely to be antipolice.[102] Our drug laws create this paradox (see figure 7.1).

While Baltimore's Eastern District may be an extreme case, it highlights a system that pumps minorities into the criminal justice system. Understand the Eastern District and you understand the nexus of drugs, violence, and imprisonment. The statistics are sobering. In Washington, DC, approximately 60 percent of a cohort of black men had been arrested, one in three specifically for selling drugs.[103] In Baltimore, 56 percent of black men in the twenties are "in the system": probation, parole, jail, or prison.[104] Nationwide it's 23 percent, and half of those are behind bars.[105] One in three black men in the twenties without a high-school education is incarcerated.[106] Seventeen percent of black men have been imprisoned, and at current rates, one-third of all black men born today will enter prison during their lifetime.[107] The odds are terrible. Stop and think about this. Police officers, myself included, are quick to blame criminals for their actions. There's something to be said for individual responsibility. But can't we, as a rich and compassionate society, do better? Can't we think beyond, "do the crime, do the time"? We're standing in the hole of failed prohibition. Can't we at least stop digging?

School Daze

> What is it with the drugs? When there's shootin' or
> fightin', you don't seem to care! But when there's
> drugs, you come right away.
>
> —*A man speaking to the author at a 7–11
> convenience store*

Handcuffs define police officers and their relation to
society. Police authority comes primarily and legally
from an officer's ability to detain and arrest. People may
ask, beg, cajole, order, and even threaten, but the function
of police ultimately lies in the ". . . or else!" of a police order. In his classic 1970 article, "The Functions of Police in
Modern Society," Egon Bittner argued that police are best
understood as "distributors of coercive force." In Bittner's
time, street justice was standard operating procedure. Police were quick with a blackjack and could shoot a fleeing
felon. While police still use and like force, times have
changed. Handcuffs have replaced street justice.

In the past, police officers may have slapped a smart-
mouthed kid or beat a wife beater. There was a day, not very
long ago, when some Baltimore police officers gave minor
offenders a choice between going to jail and taking a hit or
two. Police tell me that most offenders chose an honorable
"beat and release" over the indignity and inconvenience of a
night in jail. Perhaps to the detriment of criminals, such a
choice no longer exists.

Most police aren't willing to risk their career to prove a
point. Arrests are legal. A "good thumping" isn't (especially

when caught on videotape). Police are still ready and willing to use force, they have to be, but force no longer defines the core of policing. Today, to use police parlance, force is backup. Arrests—from drug prohibition, from public drug dealing, from greater police presence, from the dehumanization of drug addicts, from police officers' desire for court overtime pay—define policing.

Just as a culture of force gave way to a culture of arrest and "zero tolerance," the arrest culture needs to evolve into something better: a culture of crime prevention, problem solving, and police discretion. As laws against jaywalking do not fill the prisons with jaywalkers, laws against drug use did not and need not fill our jails with drug users. Drugs were illegal long before drug offenders filled our prisons. Police departments should recognize the variability of arrest discretion between police officers and focus attention on the minority of officers who make the majority of arrests. To paraphrase a slogan of the National Rifle Association: drug laws don't arrest people, police arrest people.

Police management could play a role in rolling back the war on drugs. Changing institutional motivations could change an arrest-based culture. Arrest may be necessary, but they're not good. Judge officers' effectiveness by crimes prevented rather than arrests made, schedule court appearances when officers are on duty, and provide alternatives for officers to earn overtime outside of "collars for dollars" and the "9:01 Club."[1] These changes would do little at first to lessen violence or drug addiction. But reducing the number of drug-related arrests is a desirable beginning to mitigate the harms of the war on drugs. Individuals and families affected by arrests benefit immediately. Police benefit through improved relations with the community and more resources to concentrate on violent crime and terrorism. Everybody benefits from a less burdened and more efficient court and prison system.

The damage from drug prohibition war isn't just confined to poor black neighborhoods. Disturbingly President Bush uses the language of prohibition's crusaders when he asserts a tenuous link between drugs, morality, and terrorism: "If you quit drugs, you join the fight against terror in America. And above all, we must reduce drug use for one great moral reason: . . . When we fight against drugs, we fight for the souls of our fellow Americans."[2] Similarly drug seizures in the Persian Gulf serve as proxy victories against al-Qaeda and have been called a "vital part of winning the global war on terror."[3]

Like the played-out campaign linking drugs and communism, the link between drugs and terrorism is absurdly hypocritical. In 2001 the Taliban deemed opium production un-Islamic and eliminated heroin production in Afghanistan.[4] World production dropped an estimated 75 percent.[5] Yet 2001 saw *no change* in the price or purity of heroin on the streets of Baltimore. After the U.S. invasion of Afghanistan, heroin production steadily increased. It's unfortunate, but under nominal U.S. control, Afghanistan again produces a record amount of heroin, Interpol estimates more than 90 percent of the world's supply. But does it really matter? Why bother with supply-side interdiction if *invasions* have no discernible effect on price or demand?

Our priorities are absurdly and dangerously misplaced if we think the war on drugs is more important than fighting terrorists. Profits and taxes from regulated drug production could help farmers and legitimate governments. Instead, because drugs are illegal, prohibition profits fund terrorists. Legalized and regulated drugs would be no more linked to criminals and terrorists than any other form of regulated international trade.

It is time for the debate on drug prohibition to move forward. Because we tend to advocate prohibition against "evil" while we regulate and tax that which is simply "bad," we cannot let drug policy be framed as a moral crusade. The perception that drugs are evil is not *casus belli*. But if prohibitionists want to talk morals, let them defend their policy's disproportionate impact on African Americans. If our powerful nation has a moral responsibility to promote freedom, let us defend laws and actions that fail to protect those least able to protect themselves.

Alcohol prohibition, if nothing else, should have taught us how to separate the harms of drugs from the harms of prohibition. For the most part people are happy to let state and local government regulate alcohol distribution and sales. Cities and states balance the individual's right to drink with societal harms from alcohol abuse. Legal alcohol does not make alcohol an absolute good. Similarly drug legalization is not an argument in favor of drugs or unregulated chaos. Legalization is an argument against prohibition and for control and regulation. To paraphrase a Clinton, drugs should be safe, legal, and rare.

On a policy level, any effort at effective and humane drug policy will fail if we do not understand police discretion and behavior in high-drug areas. On a theoretical level, drug laws that fail to account for police behavior will increase public hostility and embitter police. Jimmy Carter said, "Penalties against possession of a drug should not be more damaging to an individual than the use of the drug itself." But damage goes far beyond the individual user and hurts innocent families and entire communities.

Rich neighbors and strong neighborhoods will not tolerate drug dealers hawking crack on the corner. Poor neighborhoods have no choice. Police can contain public drug dealing only when residents are willing to testify, parents can control their children, and police outnumber drug dealers. And since police, like school and courts, are largely funded at a local level, poor cities and towns—urban black neighborhoods and rural white areas alike—pass a tipping point where parents, police, schools, and courts are overwhelmed. It's not a matter of getting tougher. We are tough. We could give police unlimited power to search and detain. We could abolish jury trials. We could build more prisons and throw away the key. We could model our society as a big prison and we would still have a drug problem. *Prisons have drug problems.*

An innovative analysis by Eric Cadora highlights "million-dollar blocks"—individual city blocks where more than one million dollars per block per year are spent to incarcerate individuals from that block.[6] Some blocks cost over five million dollars per year. Cadora does not question the justness of these incarcerations. But he does suspect there may be better ways to spend these criminal-justice dollars. A million dollars, coincidentally, is roughly what it would cost to pay for one patrol officer, twenty-four hours a day, every day for one year. Would the full-time presence of one officer be able to prevent the crime that leads to one-million dollars of incarceration? We could find out.

A successful drug policy should be measured in three ways. The primary goal must be the preservation of life.

Drugs are dangerous. Drug policy must not increase this danger. Preventable overdoses are the ultimate failure of prohibition. Overdoses are not an inevitable result of drug use. Nobody *wants* to overdose. With regards to drug-related violence, it is disingenuous to blame drugs for prohibition's violence. Advocates of the war on drugs have been preaching the same failed arguments for well over a century. The words and ideas of the Temperance Movement—salvation, moral ruin, crime, violence, a dangerous social class—are prohibitionists' ammunition. Imposed on an unwilling populace, prohibition is doomed to failure. The invisible hand of the market is too strong.

The second goal of drug policy should be to reduce incarceration. Just as decreasing violence in a small number of high-crime neighborhoods in the late 1990s significantly lowered the violent crime rate in the United States overall, a focus on police discretion in a limited number of high-drug neighborhoods could dramatically reduce arrests and imprisonment for the nation as a whole. Before prohibition, drug use was a matter of personal responsibility and abuse was a family, medical, or moral issue. Prohibition makes user criminals, delegates moral responsibility to police, and lets criminals profit from drug sales. Prison for nonviolent offenders is absurd. Drug regulation would reduce violent offences just as Prohibition's repeal ended bootlegging violence. Legalization would reduce the number of people we need to imprison.

The third goal, related to the second, is simply financial. While prohibition prevents us from knowing the size of the illegal drug market, one government study estimates a retail market of sixty-six billion dollars.[7] We could save additional billions simply by not funding the drug war: twenty billion at the federal level and more at the state and local levels.[8] At a cost of $22,000 per prisoner per year, drug offenders—and this ignores drug-*related* crimes—cost eight billion dollars annually.[9] The saying attributed to Senator Everett Dirksen comes to mind: "A billion here. A billion there. And pretty soon you're talking real money." Taxing marijuana as we tax alcohol and tobacco is the quickest way to take money from criminals and give it back to the public. And taxes could actually raise the cost of drugs, something the drug war, despite great effort, has failed to do.

No single best policy can cover all drugs. We have and need a myriad off laws and regulations for all the drugs already legal and prescribed. Some drugs—heroine, crack, crystal meth, inhalants—are so addictive or harmful that any use should be discouraged. Other drugs, such as marijuana and ecstasy, are not physically addictive. For these drugs, care should be taken to address issues of psychological dependency. Drugs with potential medical benefits—marijuana, ecstasy, prescription painkillers, antidepressants, Ritalin, and Viagra—need to be available to doctors and researchers.

We could learn from our successes. Tobacco policy has been surprisingly effective at reducing drug use. Regulation, taxation, and education have cut cigarette smoking in half over four decades. And not a single nicotine addict has been jailed. We changed our country's culture toward cigarette smoking. It took effort and did cost money. But most of the money came from legally taxed revenue and the cigarette companies. High taxation discourages new users from starting. Public service messages tell the truth (mostly) about the harms of tobacco. Not only is this a great victory for public health, it is perhaps our country's only success against any popular addictive drug. Drug policies could follow a similar approach: tax drug sales; treat drug abuse as a medical and social problem; set realistic goals of reduced drug use; and allow localities control over their own drug policies.

Simply decriminalizing possession is not enough. Legalization must not allow armed drug-dealing thugs to operate with impunity. In 1976, the Netherlands decriminalized possession of marijuana with the intended purpose of separating the "soft drugs" of cannabis from the "hard drugs" of cocaine and heroin.[10] This hard/soft distinction was designed to limit marijuana smokers' interaction with criminals, hard drugs, and guns. While most other drugs remain illegal, absent other criminal activity, drug addiction in the Netherlands is treated as a health issue and not a law-enforcement problem. In Amsterdam, an adult may walk into a marijuana bar, euphemistically called a "coffee shop," and proudly buy or smoke marijuana and hashish.

When I conducted research with police in Amsterdam in 1998, I saw a police office give an addict back his heroin when the addict was released after a night in jail for some petty crime. I expressed my amazement to the officer that he could give illegal drugs back to a criminal. He explained to me that as soon as the man ran out of heroin, he would break into a car to get money to buy his next hit. It made no sense to the police officer to hasten the addict's next criminal act by taking away his drugs. I asked about sending the wrong message. The police office said his message was stop breaking into cars. The Dutch police officer, no fan of drugs, thought it very strange that in a country as violent as America, police were so obsessed with jailing drug addicts.

The key to the general success of the Netherlands's marijuana policy is the regulation of drug selling. There are a limited number of "coffee shops," 250 in Amsterdam and 500 more in the rest of the nation. Police rarely have problems inside any coffee shop. Coffee shops are regulated, cannot advertise cannabis, and may be shut down by the authorities without appeal. Member of the Union of Cannabis Retailers—legalized and regulated drug dealers—are businessmen and women who pay rent and settle disputes civilly.

There is some drug tourism in Holland, but decriminalization has not led to a nation of stoners. Whatever reasons people have to get high or stay sober, legality is apparently rather far down on the list. Smoking marijuana in the Netherlands is still generally considered low-class, often associated with tourists, immigrants, or the artsy crowd. Legal weed has not lessened the stigma of drug use. While one *may* walk down the street in Amsterdam smoking a joint, it would be the equivalent of walking through an American downtown drinking from a vodka bottle. Just because you *can* do something doesn't mean you will.

The Dutch experience also helps refute the strongest argument against drug legalization: that decriminalization would dramatically increase consumption. After thirty years of regulated cannabis in the Netherlands, marijuana usage rates are *half* that found in the United States.[11] Similarly, and despite the availability of clean needles, the Netherlands has one-third as many heroin addicts per capita as does the United States. The Netherlands also spends less money on the criminal justice system, has lower levels of overall violence, fewer overdoses, and an incarceration rate one-seventh of the United States.

Of course, the United States and the Netherlands are two different countries with two different cultures, histories, and legal traditions. What works in the Netherlands may not work in the United States.[12] But it seems willfully foolish to ignore or condemn Dutch drug policy without learning from their experience. While the Dutch may not have all the answers, clearly they're doing *something* right. Yet former drug czar Barry McCaffrey called Dutch drug policy an "unmitigated disaster."[13] That only makes sense if drug policy is prohibition. The realities of Dutch drug policy are indeed a disaster for the cause of prohibition. At some point we have to accept drugs. Until then, we live with drugs *and* violence. Like Sisyphus's eternal effort pushing a rock uphill, the war on drugs is at times heroic. But more often it is simply absurd. After all these years, if the war on drugs were winnable, it would already be won.[14]

The nightly news doesn't tell you how many people die each day because of drug prohibition or highlight a DEA raid that comes up empty.[15] This drug war is becoming a forgotten war, part of American life. We shouldn't lock up the majority of black male high-school dropouts, we shouldn't have to urinate in a jar to get a job, and we should be ashamed to jail doctors. If we believe that the status quo is inevitable, if we forget history, then we risk entering a new dark age.[16] The war on drugs is a war of choice, not necessity. It's time for a better choice.

Police officers typically do not choose to work midnights in the Eastern. Such is what working people do to provide for their families. It can be demoralizing. One colleague said, "I've given up helping people. I tried that. Then I learned that things were really fucked up out there. You know, no one is going to believe you when you say how fucked up everything is." I said, "I knew things were fucked up. I just now realize that I don't want to deal with it every day." But I couldn't have written this book based on policing in Princeton, New Jersey; Scarsdale, New York; Kenilworth, Illinois; or even Northern Baltimore. Drug prohibition confines public drug dealing to poor neighborhoods.

After a year on the street, my learning curve flattened out. I handled just about every kind of call you could think of. And though every call is different, they became more and more the same. Very quickly, people with less experience than me joined the squad. Suddenly I was other people's mentor, telling them how to handle calls and helping them write reports. The job became routine. My notes became shorter and shorter. I went in for 11:39 PM roll call, hit the streets, cleared corners, settled domestics, heard gunshots, schemed consecutive days off, swapped war stories at the bar, and went to sleep around noon.

I wondered about exiting from the police department, but there was no rush. I didn't love policing but I liked it more than some. My biweekly paycheck was up to $1,100. If I stayed five years, I could get a 10 percent pension, maybe $3,500-a-year for life. If I did twenty years, I could go out with a full pension. But I knew that after eighteen more years, I would be bitter and burnt out, counting the hours toward retirement. An observant friend, admirably unburnt out despite more than thirty years on the force, said, "You know what it is about you, you don't have quite the something to be a cop. I mean, it's not that you're not a good cop, but you don't have that feeling in your heart that will make you love it. . . . You enjoy the social part of the job, the drinking and the bullshitting." He was right.

After fourteen months on the street, I had civil service protection. Barring the proverbial dead girl or live boy, my job was secure. Once they couldn't fire me, I quit. I liked knowing I could stay on the job, but that I didn't have to. I knew I could handle the ghetto, but I didn't want to. On April 1, 2001, I turned in my papers requesting unpaid leave beginning in July. If things didn't work out at school, I had one year to come back. But I heard my veteran friend when he assessed my PhD potential and future job prospects: "You better not come back here. I know that if you do, then you're a failure." I do go back, but just to see friends and eat crabs.

On my last night of work, I was sent home right after roll call. Such is tradition. Nobody wants to die on their last night of work or be responsible for someone who does. Why tempt the fates? Later that morning, my sergeant and his wife threw me a going-away party. The next day I was packed and driving back to Boston and graduate school. On the way out of Baltimore, I turned in my gun, my equipment, most of my uniform, and my uniform badge. It was a month before I could use the past tense and tell somebody I "was" a police officer. It was almost a year before I took my wallet badge out of my wallet. It would take three years to turn my field notes into a PhD dissertation and another three years teaching at John Jay College to write this book.

Meanwhile in the Eastern District, life goes on. My squadmates tell me that since I've left, things have only gotten worse. I doubt that. But that's what cops say. It's funny to hear my days already becoming as the good ol' days. I don't think they were. But who am I to say? Heeding the advice of one police officer, I've simply tried to present my experience honestly and in good faith: "You're out here. You know what it's like, what we deal with. Go tell people what we have to deal with. Spread the word. Not that anybody will believe you, of course. But maybe they'll give us a raise."

Notes

CHAPTER 1: THE DEPARTED

1. Moskos forthcoming.

2. "Two Shades of Blue" (Moskos forthcoming) offers a more thorough look at police socialization, with a focus on the differences between white and black police officers.

3. Rubinstein 1973; Friedmann 1992; and Bouza 1990.

4. Young 1991; Manning 2001.

5. Punch 1979, 4.

6. Van Maanen 1988.

7. Baltimore City and the Baltimore City police are distinct from the police and surrounding suburbs of Baltimore County. My Baltimore references refer to Baltimore City.

8. I put quotes around "passed" because I believe it is pretty easy to "pass" the Massachusetts police civil service police exam. That way, everybody who is called back can be considered "fully qualified." But without the bonus points granted various vested interest groups (such as veterans, children of police officers, and some minorities), I don't think I ever stood a chance. Apparently, and luckily for me, the standards of admission at Princeton and Harvard are more lax.

9. My starting Baltimore Police salary in 1999 was $28,400 a year. I quit after twenty months making $32,000. The starting salary in 2007 is $39,000 per year.

10. See Travis (2005) and Petersilia (2003) for more on prisoner reentry, the growingly important issue on how to best reintegrate prisoners into society after they are released from prison.

11. Everything in this book is true; nothing is fictionalized. Only names and addresses have been changed. My link with gonzo journalism is simply that I want to write in a *style* that appeals to the broadest interests. For style, I love reading Malcome Gladwell and Jane Jacobs. I am inspired by those living

198 Notes to Chapter 1

legends of academia who know how to write a good story: Anderson, Becker, Bourgois, Conley, Duneier, Jacobs (Bruce *and* Jim); Levitt, Manning, Patterson, Punch, Skolnick, Van Maanen, and Venkatesh.

The limitations and benefits of qualitative research in the sociological and anthropological fields have been expertly explained by others far better than I could ever explain myself. Among theory pieces, Duneier 1992, chapter 9, Bourgois 1995, introduction, and Jacobs and Wright 2006, chapter 1, stand out. To them, I simply tip my cap and add the richness of my data.

12. The fictional accounts in the excellent HBO miniseries *The Wire*, much of which was filmed in Baltimore's Eastern District, provide largely accurate depictions of policing and the drug trade, at least from a police perspective.

Police officers have written worthy first-hand accounts of policing, many are collected in Willis Clint's (2002) excellent anthology, *NYPD: Stories of Survival From The World's Toughest Beat*. Joseph Poss and Henry Schlesinger's first-hand description of the ghetto cop is second to none for both accuracy and entertainment.

Former Seattle Police Chief Norm Stamper's (2005) *Breaking Rank* provides a rare and honest perspective from the top of a police department.

Edward Conlon, writing in the *New Yorker* under his nom de plume, Marcus Laffey, is noteworthy for highlighting aspects of policing rarely discussed, even among police. I particularly like the relationship between an arresting officer and a prisoner described as a blind date.

Two of the best academic first-hand books on policing are: Jonathan Rubinstein's (1973) *City Police* and Malcolm Young's (1991) *An Inside Job*.

13. Eastern District census data were compiled by the author from http://factfinder.census.gov. The Eastern District includes all or parts of census tracts: 501, 603, 604, 605, 701, 702, 703, 704, 802, 803.01, 803.02, 804, 805, 806, 807, 808, 908, 909, 1001, 1002, 1004, 1203, 1204, 1205, and 2604.04.

14. The department has since upgraded to forty-five-caliber rounds with greater "stopping power."

15. For issues relating to researchers exploiting the ghetto for their own uses, see Wacquant 1997 and Elijah Anderson's 2002 response.

16. My reading list includes: *Tally's Corner* by Elliot Liebow, *The Social Order of the Slum* by Gerald Suttles, *Street Corner Society* by William Whyte, *Urban Villagers* by Herbert Gans, *The Death and Life of Great American Cities* by Jane Jacobs, *In Search of Respect* by Philippe Bourgois, *Code of the Street* and *Streetwise* by Elijah Anderson, *No Shame in My Game* by Katherine Newman, *Sidewalk* and *Slim's Table* by Mitchell Dunier, *American Apartheid* by Douglas Massey, *The Truly Disadvantaged* by William Wilson, *Nickel and Dimed* by Barbara Ehrenreich, and *The Corner* by David Simon and Edward Burns.

CHAPTER 2: BACK TO SCHOOL

1. Calling the academy "bullshit" brings to mind John Van Maanen's more thorough description of a police academy thirty-five years ago. A veteran officer tells him, "I hope the academy didn't get to you. It's something we all have to go through. A bunch of bullshit as far as I can tell . . . You'll find out mighty fast that [out here] ain't nothing like they tell you at the academy" (1973, 412).

2. In the eight years since graduation, at least 10 percent of my classmates have been fired or forced to quit for ethical or criminal violations.

3. See Hughes's 1958 *Men and Their Work*, for a discussion of "reality shock."

4. Survey data come from a sixty-five-item questionnaire administered to my class of fifty police recruits (twenty-five whites and twenty-five African American; thirty-seven men and thirteen women—the most women ever in a single academy class). This panel survey was given three times: at the beginning of the police academy, at the end of the police academy

twenty-three weeks later, and a third time after a year on the street (n=45, 50, and 34, respectively for t=1, 2, and 3). The overall response rate was 86 percent.

The first section of the survey establishes basic background demographic characteristics. The heart of the survey probes respondents' attitudes on a variety of issues including social networks, organizational solidarity, and the role of police in society. Questions on friendship networks came from the General Social Survey; questions on organizational solidarity came from Van Maanen's (1972) Questionnaire B; questions on general police issues came from a survey I previously administered to Dutch police in 1998. At t=2 and t=3, a supplement on racial attitudes was added to the survey.

While the first two stages of the questionnaire occurred in the closed environment of the police academy, the final stage (t=3) necessitated tracking down individual subjects at their respective work districts. While, many subjects expressed a strong aversion to completing questionnaires, no individual refused to complete the questionnaire when asked in person. Some subjects, due to days off and other factors, could not be located. A copy of the questionnaire with a stamped return envelope was mailed to the work address of those I could not locate in person. None of these mail-in questionnaires were returned.

5. Based on questionnaire data.

6. Westley 1953.

7. See "The Quasi-Military Organization of the Police," 136–47 in Bittner's (1970) "The Functions of Police in Modern Society."

8. Herbert 2006, 105.

9. For an example regarding radio communication, see Manning 1997, 262.

10. Freilich and Schubert 1991.

11. Almost one-third of Baltimore arrestees self-report themselves as heroin addicts. Cassie 2006.

12. Exceptions to the warrant requirement include: Exigent circumstances, flight risk, preservation of evidence, plain view,

thermal imaging, incident to arrest, motor vehicles, and public places. Most of these exceptions result from alcohol- and drug-prohibition court cases.

13. The lowering of morale was evident in both qualitative methods and statistically significant quantitative survey data.

CHAPTER 3: NEW JACK

1. Goffman 1967, 70.

2. Text in brackets is not from the original notes.

3. A questionnaire was administered three times to one academy class in 1999, 2000, and 2001. The question asked, "What's the most important reason you want to be a cop?" and asks respondents to circle one of six possible answers.

4. Motivations for becoming a police officer were different for whites and blacks. In general, white officers, disproportionately young and male, were drawn to the perceived action of the job. Black officers were more likely to express a desire to help their community and, especially among single mothers, value job benefits and job stability. The morale of white officers decreased significantly during the police academy and after the first year on the street while the morale of black officers remained almost constant (a statistically insignificant decrease).

Differences in attitudes between white and black police officers are examined in more detail in Moskos (forthcoming), "Two Shades of Blue: Racial Distinctions within a Police Identity."

5. Conspiracy and RICO laws—originally intended for the Mob but now applied to everything from music piracy to drug dealing—could convict a group a group of people planning criminal activity. But these laws are hard to prosecute and not tools of patrol officers.

6. *Baltimore Sun* 2002. Because of increased funding, the number of drug addicts in treatment has increased to 25,000.

7. Bogira 2005.

8. *Baltimore Sun* 2007. The Circuit Court ("circus court" to police) is the second tier of justice. The entry-level District Court deals with the majority of cases.

CHAPTER 4: THE CORNER

1. One arrest for every two people does not mean that every other person is arrested each year. There are a lot of repeat customers. Out of 108,000 arrests overall in Baltimore in 2005, there were 60,000 "unique individuals" (Greg Warren, director of substance-abuse treatment services for the Maryland Department of Public Safety and Correctional Services quoted in Ron Cassie's March 22, 2006, Baltimore City Paper, "High and Inside.").

If the city ratio held true for the Eastern District, it would mean that 30 percent of residents get arrested each year. Though almost assuredly, given the large number of arrests for minor charges in the Eastern District, the percentage of individuals arrested multiple times is higher in the Eastern District than in the city overall.

2. Based on my own observations and Warner and Coomer's (2003) "Neighborhood Drug Arrest Rates."

3. Baltimore's homicide rate is more than seven times the national average. See Jacobs and Write (2006) for an excellent description of both why and how violence so commonly occurs within the structure and culture of public drug dealers.

4. Author's survey data.

5. Bourgois 1995; Levitt and Venkatesh 2000.

6. Compounding Baltimore's mortality level, deaths from drug overdoses, mostly heroin, have usually been on par with homicides. Various programs focused on drug addicts have lowered overdose deaths to 218 in 2005 from 310 in 2000.

7. Jacobs 2000.

8. Shift hours have changed since my research.

9. Levitt and Venkatesh 2000.

10. Jacobs 1999.

11. Chris Rock 1996. *Bring the Pain.* DVD.

12. Katz's (1988) sneaky thrills, righteous slaughter, and badass-element of committing crime.

13. Levitt and Venkatesh (2000) show an annual 7 percent death rate for those actively involved in street-level drug dealing.

A Baltimore City police officer entering the force in 1982 and retiring in 2007 would have had, roughly, a 0.7 percent chance being killed on duty during those twenty-five years.

14. More than 11.6 percent of men in the Eastern District are murdered. This is based on homicide and census data. The 2000 Eastern District population for age 15 to 34 is 5,641 (derived from 2000 block-level U.S. Census data). The official U.S. Census citywide undercount for Baltimore was 1.8 percent. I arbitrarily double this figure for the Eastern District. Adding 3.6 percent raises the sample population to 5,844. The Eastern District lost 3 percent of its population *annually* between 1990 and 2000. Following this trend (it may have even accelerated give the massive expansion of Johns Hopkins Hospital), the 2006 population would be 4,867. I keep the 2000 population figure to be more conservative with my estimation of the homicide rate.

Daily migration is not taken into account. I do not think this accounts for a large bias in either direction. All homicide victims in the Eastern District are assumed to reside in the district. Likewise no victims outside the Eastern District are assumed to come from the district.

Homicide deaths in the Eastern District between 2000 and 2006 (excluding 2003, when I could not acquire data) are, respectively: 59, 38, 61, 55, 35, and 43. The mean is 48.5 murders per year.

The demographic characteristics of homicide victims in the Eastern District are estimated from citywide, African American sex and age data. Of the city's 179 black homicide victims in 2000 age 15 to 34, 168, or 93.9 percent, were men. 78.9 percent of all black male Baltimore homicide victims are 15 to 34 (FBI UCR 2000 Homicide Supplement).

Based on these data, the average annual homicide rate for men 15 to 35 is 615 per 100,000. To put it another way, for these men, the odds of being murdered in a single year are 1 in 163. Based on the survival rate function $1-(1-r)^x$, (r=death rate and x=number of years), 11.6 percent of men are murdered during a twenty-year period.

15. Patterson 2006.

16. In Goldstein et al.'s (1997) New York study, territorial disputes accounted for more than one-third of drug-related homicides. Their overriding point, at least in New York City in 1988, is that drug-related violence is centered almost exclusively on the trade of crack cocaine in the ghetto. This conclusion is also supported by Bruce Jacobs's (2000) and Jacobs and Wright's (2006) qualitative research. While each act of violence does not stem from a drug deal, the culture of violence and retribution grows from the illegal drug trade.

17. Goldstein et al. 1997.

18. Lizotte et al. 1997.

19. Decker, Pennell, and Caldwell 1997.

20. Decker, Pennell, and Caldwell 1997.

21. Jacobs 2000.

22. The roots of some of these gangs can be traced back to the black empowerment movement in the 1960s. In the 1980s, with the rise of crack, the empowerment-based gang leadership was replaced by a younger generation focused primarily on drug profit (Venkatesh 2000).

23. Katz and Webb 2006.

24. Jacobs and Wright 2006.

25. See Jacobs 1999; Jacobs 2000; Anderson, 1999. Bourgois 1995; Simon and Burns 1997.

26. Jacobs 1999.

27. I say some of this speaking from experience.

28. *New York Times* 2003.

29. Marijuana attitudes are based on the author's survey data. Fifteen percent of incoming officers and 20 percent of the same officers after one year on the street believe that possession of small amounts of marijuana should be legal. In the 1998 General Social Survey, 29 percent of the public agrees with the statement.

One growing group dedicated to the cause of drug legalization is Law Enforcement Against Prohibition (www.leap.cc). This organization consists of police officers, prosecutors and judges who support drug regulation rather than prohibition.

30. Vollmer 1936, 111.

CHAPTER 5: 911 IS A JOKE

1. The chapter epigraph is taken from Klockars 1983.

2. This description—from multiple observations including recordings of 911 calls—is a compilation of different calls that illustrates a typical 911 call for drug dealing from beginning to end.

3. When receiving a call, the patrol officer does not know if the call originally came from 911 or 311. For police calls, it doesn't matter what number is called. Somebody is paid to answer the phone and pass calls for service to the same dispatcher.

4. Force 1972.

5. Wilson 1968.

6. Wilson and McLaren 1972.

7. Kelling et al. 1974.

8. Sherman 1983.

9. Bayley 1994.

10. Gary Cordner and Robert Trojanowicz (1992) summarized the widely cited Kansas City Preventive Patrol Experiment (Kelling et al. 1974).

11. Spelman and Brown 1981; Kelling and Coles 1996.

12. Tien et al. 1978; Bieck and Kessler 1977; Spelman and Brown 1981.

13. Baltimore Police Department 2001.

14. Sampson 2004.

15. Moskos 2007. LEEF.

16. Moskos 2007.

17. Baltimore Police Department 2001.

18. Anderson 1999.

19. Canada 1995.

CHAPTER 6: UNDER ARREST

1. Goldstein 1960; LaFave 1962; and Kadish 1962.
2. Baltimore City Code Article 19 § 25-1.
3. Moskos 2001.
4. *Baltimore Sun* 2000.
5. *Baltimore Sun* 2003.
6. *Baltimore Sun* 2000.
7. *Baltimore Sun* 2000.
8. Data come from four-week work periods and are not the exact months listed.
9. Compstat (short for "computer statistics" and also known as comstat) is an innovative concept from the NYPD. Crime statistics are analyzed quickly rather than compiled annually. Weekly meetings are held in which district commanders are put on the spot and held responsible for crime. Commanders are able to "put cops on the dots" that represent crime on the crime map. As simple as such tactics may sound, both the quick analysis of data and the idea of holding police responsible for crime were revolutionary changes that played a large part in New York City's crime drop.

In Baltimore, however, compstat had no impact on patrol and little impact on crime. Maybe it's hard for visionary leadership to filter its way through the five ranks from commissioner to patrol, but the only pressure we patrol officers felt from above was unproductive. Perhaps this is inevitable with the chain-of-command. It is unseemly to talk to anybody more than one rank apart. In a shameful waste of smart men and women with years of knowledge and experience, the job of lower ranks is to salute and follow orders. Nobody ever asked our opinion. And the military structure prevents officers from saying, "Sir, I have an idea about how we can do this better."

For instance, after September 11, 2001, an officer was assigned to the corner of Washington and Orleans to "guard the railroad tracks." He told me the story: "I told Sarge that I've been working that post for going on seven years and there ain't never been no tracks there. He says if command staff says detail someone to guard the tracks, I gotta guard the tracks. Now that's just asinine! It's one thing if they're just screwed up in that building and think there's a railroad to protect. It's another if you can't go up the chain and set them straight."

10. The link between morale and arrest statistics is also shown by Alexandre Mas (2006). In the months after police officers lose pay-related arbitration cases, arrest rates, and average sentence length decline.

11. There are only two questions I guarantee on every exam in my "Introduction to Criminal Justice" class. The first relates to the difference between "probable cause" needed for a search or arrest and the "reasonable suspicion" for a stop or frisk. The second is the conditions meriting a Miranda reading, specifically a "custodial interrogation." T.V. and movies are correct in what Miranda is. But the idea that a police officer would be making an arrest while struggling for breath and reading somebody their rights is absurd. I and other police officers probably read Miranda to less than 1 percent of arrested suspects.

12. The dilemma of race-blind police corresponds well with Harcourt's (2007) ratchet effect, whereby racially biased enforcement leads to an increasingly disproportionate effect on minorities. If blacks face a greater chance of being arrested for drug crimes, then drug crimes will become inappropriately associated with African Americans. But the dilemma of race-blind police, unlike the ratchet effect, does not depend on any race-specific policing or race-related effect of policing, only that police are focused, as they should be, on areas with greater levels of violence.

CHAPTER 7: PROHIBITION

1. Season Three of the excellent HBO series, "The Wire" provides an excellent portrayal of some of the day-to-day problems of drug markets.

2. These are the "community disorganization effects" described by Alfred Blumstein (1995).

3. Musician Mike Skinner, aka The Streets, wonderfully describes the difference between a bad drunk and a good stoner in his song, "The Irony of it All" (Original Pirate Material, 2002).

4. Matza and Patricia Morgan 2003.

5. *New York Times* 1895.

6. Weitzer 2006.

7. Boorstin 1958; Greenberg 1999.

8. Quoted in Timberlake 1963.

9 Quoted in Timberlake 1963, 151.

10. Greenberg 1999.

11. Greenberg 1999.

12. Although it never gathered more than 2.5 percent of the vote, the Prohibition Party has survived to this day as a far-right party. Like the Prohibitionist Party, the WCTU also survives, headquartered in Evanston, Illinois.

13. Timberlake 1963.

14. Timberlake 1963; Odegard 1928.

15. Timberland 1963, 179.

16. Odegard 1928.

17. Odegard 1928.

18. Merz 1930.

19. Behr 1996.

20. Maryland's "wet" senator, Millard Tydings, quoted in Tydings 1930.

21. Other zingy 1929 government Prohibition slogans are: "Let us use alcohol, not waste it"; "Use, not abuse"; "Lawmakers must not be lawbreakers"; "It takes two to make a bootlegger"; and "Give Prohibition its chance—The liquor traffic had its day."

22. Greenberg 1999.

23. Fisher 1927, 435.

24. Warburton 1932.

25. Warburton 1932.

26. Warburton 1932, 103.

27. Dills and Miron 2004; Dills, Jacobson, and Miron 2005.

28. Behr 1996.
29. Tydings 1930.
30. Warburton 1932; Behr 1996.
31. Fisher 1927.
32. Behr 1996. For more on Prohibition in New York, see Michael Lerner's (2007) Dry Manhattan.
33. Warburton 1932, 222.
34. Behr 1996.
35. Baum 2003.
36. Baum 2003.
37. Behr 1996, 172.
38. Behr 1996, 172.
39. Behr 1996, 85.
40. Behr 1996.
41. Coffey 1975, 196.
42. Captain Bill McCoy sold high-quality liquor (hence the "Real McCoy") outside U.S. territorial limits to smaller rum runners. He eventually was arrested for smuggling and sentenced to nine months in prison.
43. Towne 1923.
44. Greenberg 1999.
45. Miron 1999.
46. Behr 1996.
47. Behr 1996.
48. Greenberg 1999, 164.
49. Gebhart 1929; Tydings 1930; Mencken 1980.
50. Behr 1996, 165.
51. Behr 1996.
52. *New York Times* 1922.
53. Gebhart 1930.
54. Wooddy 1934, 94–95.
55. Greenberg 1999, 159. Despite the Fifth Amendment's prohibition against, "any person [being] subject for the same offence to be twice put in jeopardy of life or limb," U.S. v. Lanza (1922) redefined double jeopardy by stating that an individual may be tried separately by the Federal and State governments for the same crime. Carroll v. United States (1924)

allowed police with probable cause to search cars without a search warrant. Olmstead v. United States (1928), since overruled, declared that phone conversations are public since they travel over phone lines and therefore telephone wiretaps do not require a search warrant.

56. Particularly vocal against Prohibition were representatives of Chicago, New York City and State, Maryland, New Jersey, and Rhode Island.

57. In 1915, alcohol brought in $245 million into local, state, and federal coffers, about $4.6 billion in today's dollars (Anderson 1997).

58. On the Mob's involvement with and control of organized labor, see James Jacobs's (2006) *Mobsters, Unions, and Feds: The Mafia and the American Labor Movement.*

59. One such exception is Cutten's (1944) *Should Prohibition Return?*

60. Many localities and even the majority of counties in some states remain "dry" to this day.

61. *New York Times* 1914a.

62. *New York Times* 1915a.

63. Cohen 1990. Coca-Cola, ginger ale, root beer, Cheerwine, and the very concept of a "soft drink" all have their sweet roots in temperance and alcohol prohibition.

64. *New York Times* 1884.

65. *New York Times* 1885a.

66. E.g., *New York Times* 1885b; *New York Times* 1888; *New York Times* 1889.

67. *New York Times* 1901; *New York Times* 1916.

68. *New York Times* 1897.

69. *New York Times* 1903.

70. *New York Times* 1900.

71. *New York Times* 1908b. Cocaine of this era was usually described as having powdery "flakes." Interestingly this article makes a brief mention of a form of cocaine with a "small crystal 'rock-candy' form" that was perhaps a lost precursor to crack cocaine.

72. *New York Times* 1908a.

73. MacCoun and Reuter 2001.

74. *New York Times* 1915b.

75. *New York Times* 1915b.

76. *New York Times* 1919a.

77. *New York Times* 1919b.

78. *New York Times* 1919c; MacCoun, Robert, and Reuter 2001.

79. *New York Times* 1914b.

80. *New York Times* 1920.

81. Densten 1917.

82. *New York Times* 1914a.

83. *New York Times* 1915a.

84. *New York Times* 1915a.

85. *New York Times* 1928. In 1916, two years after the unit's founding, the chief of the drug squad, Captain Henry Scherb, was awarded commendation for his work in suppression of the drug sellers (*New York Times* 1917a). His salary was raised to $1,250 or $21,200 in 2005 dollars (*New York Times* 1917b). Scherb evidently escaped culpability during the 1928 raid and retired as a Lieutenant in 1934, after forty-four years of police service (*New York Times* 1934). Scherb's $2,000 annual pension indicates a final salary, in 2005 dollars, of $57,000. Scherb died in 1943.

86. Courtwright 2001.

87. Miron (2003) believes that prohibition may have raised the price of cocaine 2.5 to 5 times. Counterfactually one can only wonder what the supply, demand, and production of cocaine would be without prohibition. Certainly in the unlikely event of regulation, high taxes could keep drug prices from plummeting.

88. Courtwright 2001.

89. Dermota 2007.

90. See, for example, Mosher and Yanagisako, 1991.

91. Baum 1996.

92. Robins et al. 1980. The fact that most soldiers did not inject drugs probably played a large factor in being able to stop.

93. *New York Times* 1914b.
94. *New York Times* 1986a.
95. *New York Times* 1986b.
96. Venkatesh 2000.
97. Reinarman and Levine 1997.
98. Fox 2000; Blumstein 2000.
99. Fox 2000.
100. Harrison and Beck 2006.
101. Schlosser 1998.
102. Carr, Napolitano, and Keating's 2007 "We Never Call the Cops and Here is Why," demonstrates the paradox of refusing to cooperate with law enforcement and yet simultaneously wanted more (or at least better) law enforcement.
103. Saner, MacCoun, and Reuter 1995, 337–62 and table 5, 356. The cohort of black men was born between 1962 and 1967. Western 2006, 3.
104. Miller 1992a. In Washington, DC, the comparable figure is 42 percent (Miller 1992b).
105. Mauer 1990.
106. Western 2006.
107. Bonczar 2003. The comparable figure for men born today is 7 percent.

EPILOGUE: SCHOOL DAZE

1. Within the Commonwealth of Massachusetts, there is a much-maligned law requiring a uniformed police officer at all road construction sites. While this is certainly feather-bedding of a sort, this law probably does wonders at reducing for-profit arrests. It is certainly better to pay police officers overtime to stand in uniform on the street than it is to pay the same officers to sit in a courthouse awaiting another postponement.
2. Bush, George W. 2001. "President Empowers Communities in Fight Against Illegal Drug Abuse: Remarks by the President in Signing Drug-Free Communities Act Reauthori-

zation Bill." White House Office of the Press Secretary. December 14.

3. *BBC News*, World Addition Online. 2003.

4. White House's Office of National Drug Control Policy. Though inventory remained, the world's major supplier of heroin produced almost no heroin.

5. ONDCP Drug Policy Information Clearing House. Drug Data Summary, March 2003.

6. Approximately thirty-three people at a rate of $30,000 per person per year.

7. Office of National Drug Control Policy 2000.

8. The White House 2002; The White House 2006. In an accounting sleight-of-hand I believe related to the Department of Homeland Security, the federal drug enforcement budget in 2002 is $18 billion annually. In 2004, the budget is listed at $12 billion, but the same publication states an increase in budget from 2002.

9. Harrison and Beck 2006. Drug offenders are 20 percent of state prisoners and 55 percent of federal prisoners.

10. Blankenburg and Bruinsma 1994.

11. U.S. Department of Health and Human Services (HHS), Substance Abuse and Mental Health Services Administration, National Household Survey on Drug Abuse: vol. 1, 109, table H1. Trimbos Institute, "Report to the EMCDDA by the Reitox National Focal Point, The Netherlands Drug Situation 2002," 28, table 2.1.

12. The "liberal" drug policy is not universally popular. Foreigners are often surprised to find that the Netherlands is a rather conservative country (one should not assume tolerance to be the sole propriety of liberals). Many in the Netherlands believe that their drug policy has gone too far, and look toward the United States for lessons in police tactics and crime prevention. But the drug-policy debate centers more on the regulation of "coffee shops" and the categorization of drugs such as ecstasy and magic mushrooms as "hard" or "soft." Nobody seriously advocates shutting down coffee shops and jailing individuals for smoking joints.

13. *Washington Post* 2005. McCaffrey falsely claimed high-crime rates in the Netherlands. Faced with criticism, McCaffrey lessened his criticism of Dutch drug policy from "unmitigated" to a "mitigated disaster."

14. Some may argue that the war has been successful, given the crime drop of the past fifteen years. In 1993 there were 24,500 murders in the United States; in 2004 there were 16,100. This decline means that there are more than 8,000 Americans every year who are not being killed. Even with the decline in murders, the homicide rate in the United States is still two to three times the rate of European countries and Canada. In 2005, Toronto, Canada, had a record high number of homicides. The same year, Chicago, slightly larger than Toronto, had a record low number of homicides. So while Toronto officials were publicly wringing their hands over their rise in violence, Chicagoans were pleased that their city has finally caught up with the national decline in violence. The numbers: seventy-four murders in Toronto; 447 in Chicago. Clearly, with regards to the crime drop in America, there is a still a long way to go. While the homicide rate in America *may* not drop any further, there is no good reason to believe that murder has bottomed out and *cannot* drop further.

15. The Cato Institute provides an excellent interactive map: "Botched Paramilitary Police Raids: An Epidemic of 'Isolated Incidents.'" Avaliable at: http://www.cato.org/raid-map/.

16. Jacobs 2004.

Bibliography

Adorno, Theodor W., Else Frenkel-Brunswik, Daniel J. Levinson, and R. Nevitt Sanford. 1964. *The Authoritarian Personality*. New York: John Wiley and Sons, Inc.

Agar, Michael, and Heather Schacht Reisinger. 2002. "A Heroin Epidemic at the Intersection of Histories: The 1960s Epidemic among African Americans in Baltimore." *Medical Anthropology* 21:189–230.

Anderson, Elijah. 1990. *Streetwise*. Chicago: The University of Chicago Press.

————. 1999. *Code of the Street*. New York: W. W. Norton & Company, Inc.

————. 2002. "The Ideologically Driven Critique." *American Journal of Sociology* 107 (6).

Anderson, Gary M. 1997. "Bureaucratic Incentives and the Transition from Taxes to Prohibition." In *Taxing Choice: The Predatory Politics of Fiscal Discrimination*, edited by William F. Shughard II. New Brunswick, NJ: Transaction Publishers.

Annual Report of the Police Commissioner for the City of Boston. 1908. Boston: Wright and Potter.

Austin, James, Marino A. Bruce, Leo Carroll, Patricia L. McCall, and Stephen C. Richards. 2001. "The Use of Incarceration in the United States." *Critical Criminology* 10:17–41.

Ball, John C. 1991. "The Similarity of Crime Rates among Male Heroin Addicts in New York City, Philadelphia and Baltimore." *Journal of Drug Issues* 21(2):413–27.

Baltimore Sun. 2000. "Quick pleas of guilty urged to unclog courts: Prosecutors seek fundamental changes in city justice system." By Caitlin Francke. November 1.

Baltimore Sun. 2002. "Drug-tied ER Visits Decline in Area: City improves to 5th from 3rd in U.S. survey; 'This is not a one-year fluke.'" By Jonathan Bor. August 30.

———. 2003. "City drops charges against Bundly." By Allison Klein. July 30.

———. 2007. "A 'Broken' System Scrutinized: Previous handling of suspect in officer's killing draws criticism of justice in the city." By Gus G. Sentementes and Annie Linskey. January 11.

———. 2007. "City man dies after Taser used to subdue him." By Gus G. Sentementes. May 15.

Banton, Michael. 1964. *The Policeman in the Community.* New York: Basic Books.

Baum, Dan. 1996. *Smoke and Mirrors: The War on Drugs and the Politics of Failure.* New York: Little, Brown and Company.

———. 2003. "Jake Leg: How the Blues diagnosed a medical mystery." *New Yorker.* September 15.

Bayley, David H. 1994. *Police For the Future.* New York: Oxford University Press.

Bayley, David H., and Harold Mendelsohn. 1969. *Minorities and the Police: Confrontation in America.* New York: The Free Press.

BBC News, World Addition Online. 2003. "US 'seizes al-Qaeda drugs ship.'" Available at: http://news.bbc.co.uk/2/hi/middle_east/3335183.stm. December 19.

Beck, Allen J., and Christopher J. Mumola. 1999. *Prisoners in 1998.* Bureau of Justice Statistics. Washington, DC: U.S. Department of Justice. August.

Becker, Howard S., Blanche Geer, Everett C. Hughes, and Anselm L. Strauss. 1961. *Boys in White: Student Culture in Medical School.* Chicago: The University of Chicago Press.

Behr, Edward. 1996. *Prohibition: Thirteen Years that Changed America.* New York: Arcade Publishing.

Bennett, Richard R., and Greenstein Theodore. 1975. "The Police Personality: A Test of the Predispositional Model." *Journal of Political Science and Administration* 3(4): 439–45.

Bieck, William, and David A. Kessler. 1977. *Response Team Analysis.* Kansas City, MO: Board of Police Commissioners.

Bittner, Egon. 1967. "The Police on Skid Row." *American Sociological Review* 32(5): 699–715.

————. 1970. "The Functions of the Police in Modern Society." *National Institute of Mental Health, Crime and Delinquency Issues Series.* Rockville, MD: Center for Studies of Crime and Delinquency.

Black, Donald J., and Albert J. Reiss, Jr. 1970. "Police Control of Juveniles." *American Sociological Review* 35:63–77.

Blankenburg, Erhard, and Freek Bruinsma. 1994. *Dutch Legal Culture.* 2nd ed. Deventer, Netherlands and Cambridge, MA: Kluwer Law and Taxation Publishers.

Blumer, Herbert. 1969. *Symbolic Interaction.* Englewood Cliffs, NJ: Prentice-Hall, Inc.

Blumstein, Alfred. 1995. "Violence by Young People: Why the Deadly Nexus?" *National Institute of Justice Journal* (August): 2–9.

————. 2000. "Disaggregating the Violence Trends." In *The Crime Drop in America*, edited by Alfred Blumstein and Joel Wallman. 11–44. New York: Cambridge University Press.

Bonczar, Thomas P. 2003. "Prevalence of Imprisonment in the U.S. Population, 1974–2001." U.S. Department of Justice Statistics, Bureau of Justice Statistics. NCJ 197976. August.

Boorstin, Daniel J. 1958. *The Americans: The Colonial Experience.* New York: Vintage Books.

Bogira, Steve. 2005. *Courtroom 302.* New York: Alfred A. Knopf.

Bopp, William J. 1977. *"O.W.": O.W. Wilson and the Search for a Police Profession.* Port Washington, NY: Kennikat Press Corp.

Bourgois, Philippe. 1995. *In Search of Respect.* New York: Cambridge University Press.

Bouza, Anthony C. 1990. *The Police Mystique: An Insider's Look at Cops, Crime, and the Criminal Justice System.* New York: Plenum Press.

Bratton, William. 1998. *Turnaround: How America's Top Cop Reversed the Crime Epidemic.* New York: Random House.

Brown, Michael K. 1981. *Working the Street: Police Discretion and the Dilemmas of Reform.* New York: Russell Sage Foundation.

Burbeck, Elizabeth, and Adrian Furnham. 1985. "Police Officer Selection: A Critical Review of the Literature." *Journal of Police Science and Administration* 13(1):58–59.

Bureau of Narcotics. 1964. "History of Narcotic Addiction in the United States." Senate Committee on Government Operations, Organized Crime and Illicit Traffic in Narcotics, 88th Congress, 1st and 2nd session. Washington, DC: U.S. Treasury Department.

Bureau of Prohibition, Education and Statistics. 1929. *How Shall We Teach the 18th Amendment?* Washington, DC: U.S. Government Printing Office.

Canada, Geoffrey. 1995. *Fist Stick Knife Gun: A Personal History of Violence in America.* Boston: Beacon Press.

Carlson, Helena, Robert E. Thayer, and A. C. Germann. 1971. "Social Attitudes and Personality Differences Among Members of Two Kinds of Police Departments (Innovative vs. Traditional) and Students." *Journal of Criminal Law, Criminology, and Political Science* 62:564–67.

Carr, Patrick J., Laura Napolitano, and Jessica Keating. 2007. "We Never Call the Cops and Here is Why: A Qualitative

Examination of Legal Cynicism in Three Philadelphia Neighborhoods." *Criminology* 45(2).

Cassie, Ron. 2006. "High and Inside." *Baltimore City Paper.* March 22.

Clark, Ronald, and Mike Hough. 1984. *Crime and Cost Effectiveness.* London: Home Office, Research Study 79.

Cadora, Eric (with Charles Swartz and Mannix Gordon). 2004. "Criminal Justice and Health and Human Services: An Exploration of Overlapping Needs, Resources, and Interests in Brooklyn Neighborhoods." In *Prisoners Once Removed: The Impact of Incarceration and Reentry on Children, Families, and Communities,* edited by Jeremy Travis and Michelle Waul. Washington, DC: Urban Institute Press.

Coffey, Thomas. 1975. *The Long Thirst: Prohibition in America, 1920–1933.* New York: W.W. Norton & Co.

Cohen, Peter. 1990. *Drugs as a Social Construct.* Dissertation. Amsterdam, Netherlands: Universiteit van Amsterdam.

Colman, Andrew M., and L. P. Gorman. 1982. "Conservatism, Dogmatism and Authoritarianism in British Police Officers." *Sociology* 16:1–11.

Conlon, Edward. 2004. *Blue Blood.* New York: Riverhead.

Cordner, Gary W., and Robert C. Trojanowicz. 1992. "Patrol." In *What Works in Policing?: Operations and Administration Examined,* edited by Gary W. Cordner and Donna C. Hale, 3–18. Cincinnati, OH: Anderson Publishing Co.

Courtwright, David T. 2001. *Dark Paradise: A History of Opiate Addiction in America.* Cambridge, MA: Harvard University Press.

Cowen, Jacqueline, and Jens Ludwig. 2003. "Policing Crime Guns." In *Evaluating Gun Policy,* edited by Jens Ludwig and Philip Cook, 217–39. Washington, DC: Brookings.

Critchley, T. A. 1967. *A History of Police in England and Wales 900–1966.* London: Constable and Company Ltd.

Cutten, George B. 1944. *Should Prohibition Return?* New York: Fleming H Revell.

Davis, Kenneth Culp. 1975. *Police Discretion.* St. Paul, MN: West Publishing Co.

Davis, James A., Tom W. Smith, and Peter V. Marsden. 2003. General Social Surveys, 1972–2002: [Cumulative File] [Computer file]. ICPSR version. Chicago, IL: National Opinion Research Center [producer], 2003. Storrs, CT: Roper Center for Public Opinion Research, University of Connecticut/Ann Arbor, MI: Inter-university Consortium for Political and Social Research [distributors].

Decker, Scott. 2003. *Policing Gangs and Youth Violence.* Belmont, CA: Wadsworth.

Decker, Scott H., Susan Pennell, and Ami Caldwell. 1997. *Illegal Firearms: Access and Use by Arrestees.* Research in Brief (NCJ 163496). Washington, DC: U.S. Department of Justice, National Institute of Justice.

Dedman, Bill, and Francie Latour. 2003. "Race, Sex, and Age Drive Ticketing: Minorities and Men Least Likely to Receive Warnings." *Boston Globe.* July 20.

Densten, J. C. 1917. "Drug Addiction and the Harrison Anti-Narcotic Act." *New York Medical Journal* 105:747–48.

Dermota, Ken. 2007. "Snow Fall." *Atlantic Monthly.* July/ August.

Dills, Angela, and Jeffrey Miron. 2004. "Alcohol Prohibition and Cirrhosis." *American Law and Economic Review* 6 (2).

Dills, Angela, Mireille Jacobson, and Jeffrey Miron. 2005. "The Effect of Alcohol Prohibition on Alcohol Consumption: Evidence from Drunkenness Arrests." *Economics Letters,* 279–94.

Duneier, Mitchell. 1992. *Slim's Table.* Chicago: The University of Chicago Press.

———. 1999. *Sidewalk.* New York: Farrar, Straus & Giroux.

Economist. 2002. "All Stars, No Bars: Sobriety in Deepest Arkansas." August 10, 29.

Ehrenreich, Barbara. 2001. *Nickel and Dimed: On (Not) Getting by in America.* New York: Metropolitan Books.

Emsley, Clive. 1983. *Policing and its Context, 1750–1870.* London: Macmillan.

Engel, Robin Shepard, James J. Sobol, and Robert E. Worden. 2000. "Further Exploration Of The Demeanor Hypothesis: The Interaction Effects Of Suspects' Characteristics And Demeanor On Police Behavior." *Justice Quarterly* 17(2): 235–58.

Evans, Sara M. 1989[1997]. *Born for Liberty: A History of Women in America.* New York: Free Press.

Fisher, Irving. 1927. *Prohibition at Its Worst.* New York: Alcohol Information Committee.

Free, Marvin D., Jr. 2001. "Racial Bias and the American Criminal Justice System: Race and Presentencing Revisited." *Critical Criminology* 10:195–223.

Force, Robert. 1972. "Decriminalization of Breach of the Peace Statutes: A Nonpenal Approach to Order Maintenance." *Tulane Law Review* 46:367–493.

Fox, James Alan. 2000. "Demographics and U.S. Homicide." In *The Crime Drop in America*, edited by Alfred Blumstein and Joel Wallman, 288–317. New York: Cambridge University Press.

Freilich, Morris, and Frank A. Schubert. 1989. "Proper Rules, Smart Rules, and Police Discretion" In *The Relevance of Culture*, edited by Morris Freilich, 218–44. South Hadley, MA: Bergin and Garvey.

Friedmann, Robert R. 1992. *Community Policing: Comparative Perspectives and Prospects.* New York: Harvester Wheatsheaf.

Gans, Herbert J. 1962. *The Urban Villagers: Group and Class in the Life of Italian-American.* New York: Free Press of Glencoe.

Gebhart, John C. 1929. *Reforming America With a Shot Gun: A Study of Prohibition Killings.* Washington, DC: Association Against the Prohibition Amendment.

————. 1930. *Clogging of Courts and Prisons.* Washington, DC: Association Against the Prohibition Amendment.

Genz, John L., and David Lester. 1976. "Authoritarianism in Policemen as a Function of Experience." *Journal of Political Science and Administration* 4:9–13.

Gibbons, Mary. 2004. "Profiling—More Than a Euphemism for Discrimination: Legitimate Use of a Maligned Investigative Tool." In *Policing and Minority Communities: Bridging the Gap,* edited by Delores D. Jones-Brown and Karen J. Terry, 36–51. Upper Saddle River, NJ: Pearson Education Inc.

Gladwell, Malcolm. 1996. "The Tipping Point." *New Yorker.* June 3.

Goffman, Erving. 1967. *Interaction Ritual: Essays in Face-to-Face Behavior.* Chicago: Aldine Publishing Co.

Goldstein, Herman. 1990. *Problem-Oriented Policing.* New York: McGraw-Hill.

Goldstein, Joseph. 1960. "Police Discretion Not to Invoke the Criminal Process: Low Visibility Decisions in the Administration of Justice." *Yale Law Journal* 69:543–94.

Goldstein, Paul J. 1985. "The Drug/Violence Nexus: A Tripartite Conceptual Framework." *Journal of Drug Issues* 14:493–506.

Goldstein, Paul J., Henry H. Brownstein, Patrick J. Ryan, and Patricia A. Bellucci. 1997. "Crack and Homicide in New York City: A Case Study in the Epidemiology of Violence." In *Crack in America: Demon Drugs and Social Justice,* edited by Craig Reinarman and Harry G. Levine. Berkeley, CA: University of California Press.

Goffman, Erving. 1967. *Interaction Ritual: Essays on Face-To-Face Behavior.* New York: Anchor Books.

Goffman, Erving. 1983. "The Interaction Order." *American Sociology Review* 48:1–17.

Gray, James P. 2001. *Why Our Drug Laws Have Failed and What We can Do about It: A Judicial Indictment of the War on Drugs.* Philadelphia: Temple University Press.

Greenberg, Martin Alan. 1999. *Prohibition Enforcement: Charting a New Mission.* Springfield, IL: Charles C Thomas.

Gross, Samuel R., and Katherine Y. Bares. 2002. "Road Work: Racial Profiling and Drug Interdiction on the Highway." *Michigan Law Review* 101, 3 (December).

Gurr, Ted R. 1989. "On the History of Violent Crime in Europe and America." In *Violence in America: The History of Crime*, edited by Ted R. Gurr, 1–17. Beverly Hills, CA: Sage Publications.

Harcourt, Bernard E. 2001. *The Illusion of Order: The False Promise of Broken Windows Policing.* Cambridge, MA: Harvard University Press.

———. 2007. *Against Prediction: Profiling, Policing, and Punishing in an Actuarial Age.* Chicago: University of Chicago Press.

Harris, Leslie M. 2003. *In the Shadow of Slavery: African Americans in New York City, 1626–1863.* Chicago: The University of Chicago Press.

Harris, Richard N. 1973. *The Police Academy: An Inside View.* New York: John Wiley & Sons, Inc.

Harrison, Paige M., and Allen J. Beck. 2001. *Prisoners in 2001.* Washington, DC: U.S. Department of Justice.

———. 2005. *Prison and Jail Inmates at Midyear 2004.* Bureau of Justice Statistics. Washington, DC: U.S. Department of Justice, April.

———. 2006. *Prison and Jail Inmates at Midyear 2005.* Bureau of Justice Statistics. Washington, DC: U.S. Department of Justice, May.

Herbert, Steve. 1997. *Policing Space.* Minneapolis, MN: The University of Minnesota Press.

Herbert, Steve. 2006. *Citizens, Cops, and Power: Recognizing the Limits of Community*. Chicago: The University of Chicago Press.

Hughes, Everett C. 1958. *Men and Their Work*. Glencoe, Ill: Free Press.

Jacobs, Bruce A. 1999. *Dealing Crack: the Social World of Streetcorner Selling*. Boston: Northeastern University Press.

———. 2000. *Robbing Drug Dealers: Violence beyond the Law*. New York: Walter de Gruyter, Inc.

Jacobs, Bruce A., and Richard Wright. 2006. *Street Justice: Retaliation in the Criminal Underworld*. New York: Cambridge University Press.

Jacobs, James B. 2006. *Mobsters, Unions, And Feds: The Mafia And the American Labor Movement*. New York: New York University Press.

Jacobs, Jane. 1961. *The Death and Life of Great American Cities*. New York: Random House.

———. 2004. *Dark Age Ahead*. New York: Random House.

Johnson, David Ralph. 1979. *Policing the Urban Underworld*. Philadelphia: Temple University Press.

Jones-Brown, Delores D. 2001. "Fatal Profiles: Too Many 'Tragic Mistakes' Not Enough Justice." *New Jersey Lawyer* (February).

Kadish, Sanford H. 1962. "Local Norms and Discretion in the Police and Sentencing Processes." *Harvard Law Review* 75 (March):904–31.

Kansas City Police Department. 1977. *Response Time Analysis: Volume II—Part I Crime Analysis*. Kansas City, MO.

Karmen, Andrew. 2000. *New York Murder Mystery: The True Story behind the Crime Crash of the 1990s*. New York: New York University Press.

Katz, Charles M., and Vincent J. Webb. 2006. *Policing Gangs in America*. New York: Cambridge University Press.

Katz, Charles M., Vincent J. Webb, and David J. Webb. 2001. "An Assessment of the Impact of Quality-of-Life Policing on Crime and Disorder." *Justice Quarterly* 18 (4).

Katz, Jack. 1988. *Seductions of Crime*. New York: Basic Books.

Kelling, George L. 1985. "Order Maintenance, the Quality of Urban Life, and Police: A Line of Argument." In *Police Leadership in America*, edited by William A. Geller, 296–308. New York: Praeger Publishers.

Kelling, George L., and Catherine M. Coles. 1996. *Fixing Broken Windows*. New York: The Free Press.

Kelling, George L., Tony Pate, Duane Diekman, and Charles E. Brown. 1974. *The Kansas City Preventive Patrol Experiment: A Summary Report*. Washington, DC: National Institute of Justice.

Kennedy, David M. 1997. "Pulling Levers: Chronic Offenders, High-Crime Settings, and a Theory of Prevention." *Valparaiso Law Review*. Valparaiso, IN, 449–84.

Klinger, David A. 1997. "Negotiating Order in Patrol Work: An Ecological Theory of Police Response to Deviance." *Criminology* 35 (2):277–306.

Klockars, Carl. B., ed. 1983. *Thinking About Police*. New York: McGraw-Hill.

Koenig, Daniel J. 1991. *Do Police Cause Crime?: Police Activity, Police Strength and Crime Rates*. Ottawa: Canadian Police College.

Krahn, Harvey, and Leslie Kennedy. 1985. "Producing Personal Safety: The Effects of Crime Rates, Police Force Size, and Fear of Crime." *Criminology* 23 (4):697–710.

LaFave, Wayne R. 1962. "The Police and Non-enforcement of the Law-Part I." *Wisconsin Law Review* (January):104–37.

Laffey, Marcus. 1997. "Cop Diary." *New Yorker*. November 11.

Lange, James E., Mark B. Johnson, and Robert B. Voas. 2005. "Testing the racial profiling hypothesis for seemingly disparate traffic stops on the New Jersey Turnpike." *Justice Quarterly* 22 (2):193–223.

Lane, Roger. 1980. "Urban Police and Crime in Nineteenth-Century America." In *Crime and Justice*, edited by N. Morris and M. Tonry, 1–43. Chicago: The University of Chicago Press.

Laurie, Peter. 1970. *Scotland Yard*. New York: Holt, Rinehart and Winston.

Lerner, Michael A. 2007. *Dry Manhattan: Prohibition in New York City*. Cambridge, MA: Harvard University Press.

Levitt, Steven D. 2004. "Understanding Why Crime Fell in the 1990s: Four Factors that Explain the Decline and Six that Do Not." *Journal of Economic Perspectives* 18 (1):163–90.

Levitt, Steven D., and Sudhir Alladi Venkatesh. 2000. "An Economic Analysis of a Drug-Selling Gang's Finances." *Quarterly Journal of Economics* 115 (3):755–89.

Liebow, Elliot. 1967[1983]. *Tally's Corner: A Study of Negro Streetcorner Men*. New York: Rowman & Littlefield.

Lizotte, Alan J., Gregory J. Howard, Marvin D. Krohn, and Terence P. Thornberry. 1997. "Patterns of Illegal Gun Carrying Among Young Urban Males." *Valparaiso University Law Review* 31:375–93.

Loftin, Colin, and David McDowall. 1982. "The Police, Crime, and Economic Theory: An Assessment." *American Sociological Review* 47:393–401.

Lundman, Richard J. 2004. "Driver Race, Ethnicity, and Gender and Citizen Reports of Vehicle Searches by Police and Vehicle Search Hits: Toward a Triangulated Scholarly Understanding." *Journal of Criminal Law and Criminology* 94 (2):309–50.

Lynch, James P., and Lynn A. Addington, eds. 2007. *Understanding Crime Statistics: Revisiting the Divergence of the NCVS and UCR*. New York: Cambridge University Press.

MacCoun, Robert, and P. Reuter. 2001. *Drug War Heresies: Learning From Other Vices, Times, and Places.* New York: Cambridge University Press.

Manning, Peter K. 1977. *Police Work: the Social Organization of Policing.* Cambridge, MA: The Massachusetts Institute of Technology.

———. 1997. *Police Work: the Social Organization of Policing.* 2nd ed. Prospect Heights, IL: Waveland Press, Inc.

———. 2001. "Theorizing Policing: The Drama and Myth of Crime Control in the NYPD." *Theoretical Criminology* 5 (3):315–44.

———. 2004. *The Narcs' Game: Organizational and Informational Limits on Drug Law Enforcement.* 2nd ed. Prospect Heights, IL: Waveland Press, Inc.

Mas, Alexandre. 2006. "Pay, Reference Points, and Police Performance." *Quarterly Journal of Economics* 71 (3):783–821.

Mass, Peter. 1973. *Serpico: The Cop Who Defied the System.* New York: Viking Press.

Massey, Douglas S. 1993. *American Apartheid: Segregation and the Making of the Underclass.* Cambridge, MA: Harvard University Press.

Mastrofski, Stephen D., Jeffrey B. Snipes, Roger B. Parks, and Christopher D. Maxwell. 2000. "The Helping Hand Of The Law: Police Control Of Citizens On Request." *Criminology* 38 (2):307–42.

Matarazzo, Joseph D., Bernadene V. Allen, George Saslow, and Arthur N. Wiens. 1964. "Characteristics Of Successful Policemen And Firemen Applicants." *Journal of Applied Psychology* 48 (2):123–33.

Matza, David, and Patricia Morgan. 2003. "Controlling Drug Use: the Great Prohibition." In *Punishment and Social Control*, 2nd ed., edited by Thomas G. Blomberg and Stanley Cohen, 133–48. New York: Aldine de Gruyter.

Mauer, Marc. 1990. *Young Black Men and the Criminal Justice System: A Growing National Problem*. Washington, DC: The Sentencing Project.

McAlary, Mike. 1987. *Buddy Boys: When Good Cops Turn Bad*. New York: Putnam Press.

McGarrell, Edmund, Steven Chermak, Jeremy M. Wilson, and Nicholas Cosaro. 2006. "Reducing Homicide through a 'Lever-Pulling' Strategy." *Justice Quarterly* 23 (2):214–31.

McNamara, John. 1967. "Uncertainties in Police Work: The Relevance of Police Recruits' Background and Training." In *The Police: Six Sociological Essays*, edited by David J. Bordua, 163–252. New York: John Wiley & Sons, Inc.

Meierhoefer, Barbara S. 1992. *The General Effect of Mandatory Minimum Prison Terms: A Longitudinal Study of Federal Sentences Imposed*. Washington, DC: Federal Judicial Center, 20.

Mencken, H. L. 1941. "Recollections of Notable Cops" *Newspaper Days: 1899–1906*. New York: Alfred A. Knopf.

———. 1980. *A Choice of Days*. New York: Knopf.

Merz, Charles. 1930. *The Dry Decade*. Garden City, NY: Doubleday, Doran and Co.

Miller, Jerome G. 1992a. "56 Percent of Young Black Males in Baltimore Under Justice System Control." *Overcrowded Times* 3 (6).

———. 1992b. "42% of Black D.C. Males, 18 to 35, Under Criminal Justice System Control." *Overcrowded Times* 3 (3).

Miller, Susan L. 1999. *Gender and Community Policing: Walking the Walk*. Boston: Northeastern University Press.

Miron, Jeffrey A. 1999. "Violence and the U.S. Prohibitions of Drugs and Alcohol." *American Law Economics Review* 1 (Fall).

———. 2003. "Do Prohibitions Raise Prices: Evidence from the Market for Cocaine." *Review of Economics and Statistics* 85, 3 (August).

Morris, Pauline, and Kevin Heal. 1981. *Crime Control and the Police: A Review of Research.* London: Home Office, Research Study 67.

Mosher, James F., and Karen L. Yanagisako. 1991. "Public Health, Not Social Warfare: A Public Health Approach to Illegal Drug Policy" *Journal of Public Health Policy* 12 (3):278–323.

Moskos, Peter C. 2001. "Buckle Up or the Lock Up." *Baltimore Sun.* Op-ed. April 27.

———. 2003. "Feet on the Street." *New York Post.* Op-ed. June 23.

———. 2007. "911 and the Failure of Police Rapid Response." *Law Enforcement Executive Forum* 7 (4):137–49.

———. Forthcoming. "Two Shades of Blue: Racial Distinctions within a Police Identity."

New York Times. 1859. "The Metropolitan Police: Quarterly Report of Superintendent Pillsbury" November 19, 1.

———. 1863. "Local Intelligence: The Metropolitan Police. Superintendent Kennedy's Quarterly Report." March 26, 2.

———. 1875. "Three Months' Police Work: Quarterly Report of the Commissioners." August 6, 10.

———. 1884. "The Anaesthetic Cocaine." December 23.

———. 1885a. "Poisoned by Cocaine." November 19.

———. 1885b. "Cocaine's Terrible effect: A Chicago Physician becomes insane from using the drug." November 30, 1.

———. 1887. "Crazed by Drugs." March 8.

———. 1888. "A Victim to Cocaine." August 29.

———. 1889. "One of Cocaine's Victims." December 22, 9.

———. 1897. "Driven to Crime by Cocaine: Turned Burglar to Secure money to Purchase the Drug." March 29, 4.

———. 1898. "Died a Victim of Cocaine." February 14, 5.

———. 1895. "Pulpit and the Saloon: Prohibition the Only Cure." October 21.

New York Times. 1900. "Morphine Victims Sentenced: Four Human Wrecks Arraigned in the West Side Court." November 3, 8.

———. 1901. "Rev. E.S. Phillips Found Dead in This City." May 18, 3.

———. 1903. "Hampton Negro Conference: Alarming Spread of Cocaine Habit Among the Blacks." July 16, 2.

———. 1908a. "Cocaine Forbidden in the U.S. Mails/Government discovered that great quantities were sold direct to users/ Negroes took up habit/Pure Food Experts are on the Track of Patent Medicines Which Contain the Drug." July 15, 5.

———. 1908b. "The Growing Menace of the Use of Cocaine." August 2, SM1.

———. 1914a. "Police round up drug users here." July 15, 18.

———. 1914b. "Negro Cocaine 'Fiends' New Southern Menace; Murder and Insanity Increasing Among Lower Class Because They Have Taken To 'Sniffing' Since Being Deprived Of Whisky By Prohibition." by Edward Huntington Williams, M.D. February 8.

———. 1915a. "Woods Takes Pride in the Drug Squad/During the year its members arrested 1,950 victims or dealers/ Great Progress is Made." April 4, C4.

———. 1915b. "200,000 Drug Users In United States: Government Report Says the Number of Addicts has Been Overestimated." Oct 28, 14.

———. 1915b. "Problems of Drug Addiction." April 16.

———. 1915c. "Woods Takes Pride in the Drug Squad/During the year its members arrested 1,950 victims or dealers/ Great Progress is Made." April 4, C4.

———. 1916. "Drug users begs for mercy for victims: Tells medical editors they should have same treatment from society as drunkards." October 26, 8.

———. 1917a. "Courageous acts win police honors." January 1.

———. 1917b. "Police and Fire News." November 28, 23.

New York Times. 1919a. "Fear Outbreak by Men needing Drugs" April 10.

————. 1919b. "8,000 Lads in City are Drug Addicts." April 15.

————. 1919c. "City Sends About 135 Addicts of Both Sexes to Special Wards in Hospitals; Copeland Plans Campaign, Two Doctors, Three Druggists, and One Addict Arrested in Raid in Brooklyn." April 11.

————. 1920. "Plan National Drive Against Drug Traffic; Revenue Bureau Officials Find Alarming Increase in Victims and Prepare to Enforce Law." March 7.

————. 1922. "Orders All to Jail in Volstead Cases." December 16, 25.

————. 1928. "Four in Drug Squad Ousted." July 1.

————. 1930. "Four Seized in Drug Drive." February 1, 16.

————. 1934. "Police Department." April 13.

————. 1986a. "On City Street Corners, Night of Antidrug Vigils; Church Leaders Organize Vigils To Fight Drugs." By Gary Gately. July 22. B1.

————. 1986b. "Anatomy of the Drug Issue: How, After Years, It Erupted; Anatomy of an Issue: How, After Years, Drugs Touched a Nerve." By Peter Kerr. November 17. A1.

————. 2002a. "Pastoral Poverty: The Seeds of Decline." By Timothy Egan. December 8, 1.

————. 2002b. "Zones of Devastation From 9/11: Mapping the Victims by ZIP Code." By Andy Newman. August 21, 1.

————. 2003. "In Baltimore, Slogan Collides with Reality." By Jeffery Gettleman. September 2.

Newman, Katherine. 1999. *No Shame in My Game: The Working Poor in the Inner City.* New York: Russell Sage Foundation and Knopf.

Odegard, Peter H. 1928. *Pressure Politics: The Story of the Anti-Saloon League.* New York: Columbia University Press, 60.

Office of National Drug Control Policy. 2000. "What America's Users Spend on Illegal Drugs 1988–1999." Washington DC: The White House.

Patterson, Orlando. 2006. "A Poverty of the Mind." *New York Times.* March 26.

Petersilia, Joan. 2003. *When Prisoners Come Home: Parole and Prisoner Reentry.* New York: Oxford University Press.

Pfuhl, Erdwin, Jr. 1983. "Police Strikes and Conventional Crime." *Criminology* 21:489–503.

Piliavin, Irving, and Scott Briar. 1964. "Police Encounters with Juveniles." *American Journal of Sociology* 70:206–14.

Police Foundation. 1981. *The Newark Foot Patrol Experiment.* Washington, DC: Police Foundation.

Poss, M. Joseph, and Henry R. Schlesinger. 1994. *Brooklyn Bounce: The True-Life Adventures of a Good Cop in a Bad Precinct.* New York: Avon.

Preble, Edward. 1980. "El Barrio Revisited." Paper presented at the annual meeting of the Society of Applied Anthropology.

Punch, Maurice. 1979. *Policing the Inner City: A Study of Amsterdam's Warmoesstraat.* London: Macmillan.

Reiner, Robert. 1995. "Myth vs. Modernity: Reality and Unreality in the English Model of Policing." In *Comparisons in Policing: An International Perspective*, edited by Jean-Paul Brodeur, 16–43. Brookfield, Vermont: Ashgate Publishing Company.

Reinarman, Craig, and Harry G. Levine, eds. 1997. *Crack in America: Demon Drugs and Social Justice.* Berkeley, CA: University of California Press.

Reiss, Albert J., Jr. 1971. *The Police and the Public.* New Haven: Yale University Press.

Reith, Charles. 1948. *A Short History of the British Police.* London: Oxford University Press.

Reuss-Ianni, Elizabeth. 1983. *Two Cultures of Policing*. New Brunswick, NJ: Transaction Books.

Riksheim, Eric C., and Steven M. Chermak. 1993. "Causes of Police Behavior Revisited." *Journal of Criminal Justice*, 21:353–82.

Robins, Lee N., John E. Helzer, Michi Hesselbrock, and Eric Wish. 1980. "Vietnam Veterans Three Years After Vietnam: How Our Study Changed Our View of Heroin." In *The Yearbook of Substance Use and Abuse*, edited by. L. Brill and C. Winick, 2:213–30. New York: Human Sciences Press.

Robinson, Amanda L., and Meghan S. Chandek. 2000. "The Domestic Violence Arrest Decision: Examining Demographic, Attitudinal, And Situational Variables." *Crime & Delinquency* 46 (1):18–37.

Rowe, Thomas C. 2006. *Federal Narcotics Laws and the War on Drugs: Money Down a Rat Hole*. Binghamtom, NY: Haworth Press.

Rubinstein, Jonathan. 1973. *City Police*. New York: Farrar, Straus and Giroux.

Sampson, Rana. 2004. "Misuse of Abuse of 911." *Problem-Oriented Guides for Police. Problem-Specific Guides Series*. Guide No. 19. Washington, DC: U.S. Department of Justice.

Sampson, Robert J., and Stephen W. Raudenbush. 1999. "Systematic Social Observation of Public Spaces: A New Look at Disorder in Urban Neighborhoods." *American Journal of Sociology* 105 (3):603–51.

Saner, Hilary, Robert MacCoun, and Peter Reuter. 1995. "On the Ubiquity of Drug Selling Among Youthful Offenders in Washington, D.C., 1985–1990. *Journal of Quantitative Criminology* 11 (4):337–62.

Schlosser, Eric. 1998. "The Prison-Industrial Complex." *Atlantic Monthly*. December.

Sherman, Lawrence W. 1983. "Patrol Strategies for Police." In James Q. Wilson (ed.). *Crime and Public Policy.* San Francisco, CA: Institute for Contemporary Studies.

Silberman, Charles. 1978. *Criminal Violence, Criminal Justice.* New York: Random House.

Simon, David, and Edward Burns. 1997. *The Corner.* New York: Broadway Books.

Skogan, Wesley G. 1990. *Disorder and Decline: Crime and Spiral of Decay in America.* New York: The Free Press.

Skogan, Wesley G., and Susan M. Harnett. 1997. *Community Policing, Chicago Style.* New York: Oxford University Press.

Smith, Douglas A. 1986. "The Neighborhood Context of Police Behavior." In *Communities and Crime*, edited by Albert J. Reiss, Jr. and Michael Tonry, 313–41. (Vol. 8 of *Crime and Justice: A Review of Research*, edited by Michael Tonry and Norval Morris). Chicago: The University of Chicago Press.

Spelman, William, and Dale K. Brown. 1981. *Calling the Police: Citizen Reporting of Serious Crime.* Washington, DC: Police Executive Research Forum.

Stamper, Norm. 2005. *Breaking Rank: A Top Cop's Expose of the Dark Side of American Policing.* New York: Nation Books.

Substance Abuse and Mental Heath Services Administration, Office of Applied Studies. 2002. *Mortality Data from the Drug Abuse Warning Network, 2000.* DAWN Series D-19, DHHS Publication No. (SMA) 02-3633. Rockville, MD.

Suttles, Gerald D. 1968. *The Social Order of the Slum: Ethnicity and Territory in the Inner City.* Chicago: The University of Chicago Press.

Taylor, Ralph B. 2001. *Breaking Away from Broken Windows: Baltimore Neighborhoods and the Nationwide Fight against Crime, Grime, Fear, and Decline.* Boulder, CO: Westwood Press.

Tien, James M., James W. Simon, and Richard C. Larson. 1978. *An Alternative Approach in Police Patrol: The Wilming-*

ton Split-Force Experiment. Washington, DC: Government Printing Office.

Timberlake, James H. 1963. *Prohibition and the Progressive Movement, 1900–1920.* Cambridge, MA: Harvard University Press.

Tonry, Michael. 1995. *Malign Neglect.* New York: Oxford University Press.

Towne, Charles Hanson. 1923. *The Rise and Fall of Prohibition: The Human Side of What the Eighteenth Amendment Has Done to the United States.* New York: Macmillan.

Travis, Jeremy. 2005. *But They All Come Back: Facing The Challenges Of Prisoner Reentry.* New York: The Urban Institute.

Tydings, Millard E. 1930. *Before and After Prohibition.* New York: MacMillan.

U.S. Census Bureau. 2000. Census of Population and Housing, generated by Peter Moskos.

———. 2001. State and County QuickFacts. Data derived from Population Estimates, 2000 Census of Population and Housing, 1990 Census of Population and Housing, Small Area Income and Poverty Estimates, County Business Patterns, 1997 Economic Census, Minority- and Women-Owned Business, Building Permits, Consolidated Federal Funds Report, 1997 Census of Governments. Avaliable at: http://quickfacts.census.gov/qfd/states/24/24510.html.

U.S. Drug Enforcement Administration. 2000. *Baltimore District Report.* Washington, DC: DEA, July.

Van Maanen, John. 1972. *Pledging the Police: A Study of Selected Aspects of Recruit Socialization in a Large, Urban Police Department.* Ph.D. dissertation: University of California, Irvine.

———. 1973. "Observations on the Making of Policemen." *Human Organization* 32 (4).

———. 1976. "Breaking in: Socialization to Work." In *Handbook of Work, Organization and Society*, edited by R. Dubins. Chicago: Rand McNally.

Van Maanen, John. 1982. "Boundary Crossings: Major Strategies of Organizational Socialization and Their Consequences." In *Career Issues in Human Resource Management*, edited by Ralph Katz, 85–115. Englewood Cliffs, New Jersey: Prentice-Hall.

———. 1988. *Tales of the Field.* Chicago: The University of Chicago Press.

Venkatesh, Sudhir Alladi. 2000. *American Project: The Rise and Fall of a Modern Ghetto.* Cambridge, MA: Harvard University Press.

Vollmer, August. 1936. *The Police and Modern Society.* Berkeley: University of California Press.

Wacquant, Loïc. 1997. "Three Pernicious Premises in the Study of the American Ghetto." *International Journal of Urban and Regional Research* 20 (2):341–53.

Walker, Samuel. 1989. *Sense and Nonsense About Crime.* 2nd ed. Pacific Grove, CA: Brooks/Cole Publishing Co.

Warburton, Clark. 1932. *The Economic Results of Prohibition.* New York: Columbia University Press.

Warner, Barbara D., and Brandi Wilson Coomer. 2003. "Neighborhood Drug Arrest Rates: Are They a Meaningful Indicator of Drug Activity? A Research Note." *Journal of Research in crime and Delinquency* 40, 2 (May):123–38.

Washington Post. 2005 "U.S. and Netherlands Reach Accord on Cutting Drug Use." By Sam Coates. July 18.

Weitzer, Ronald. 2006. "Moral Crusade Against Prostitution" *Society* (March/April).

Western, Bruce. 2006. *Punishment and Inequality in America.* New York: Russell Sage Foundation.

Westley, William A. 1953 "Violence and the Police." *American Journal of Sociology* 59:34–41.

The White House. 2002. "National Drug Control Strategy–FY 2001 Budget Summary." February.

The White House. 2006. "National Drug Control Strategy–FY 2007 Budget Summary." February.

Whyte, William Foote. 1943. *Street Corner Society.* Chicago: The University of Chicago Press.

Willis, Clint, ed. 2002. *NYPD: Stories of Survival From the World's Toughest Beat.* New York: Thunder's Mouth Press.

Wilson, James Q. 1968. *Varieties of Police Behavior.* Cambridge, MA: Harvard University Press.

————. 1979. *The Effect of the Police on Crime.* Washington, DC: U.S. Department of Justice.

————, ed. 1983. *Crime and Public Policy.* San Francisco, CA: Institute for Contemporary Studies.

Wilson, James Q., and George L. Kelling. 1982. "Broken Windows: The Police and Neighborhood Safety." *Atlantic Monthly* (March):29–38.

Wilson, Orlando W. 1950. *Police Administration.* New York: McGraw-Hill.

Wilson, Orlando W., and R. McLaren. 1972. *Police Administration.* 3rd ed. New York: McGraw-Hill.

Wilson, William Julius. 1987. *The Truly Disadvantaged: the Inner City, the Underclass, and Public Policy.* Chicago: The University of Chicago Press.

Wilson, William Julius. 1996. *When Work Disappears.* New York: Random House.

The Wire. 2002–6. HBO Television Series.

Wish, Eric D., and George S. Yacoubian, Jr. 2001. *Findings from the 2001 Baltimore City Substance Abuse Need for Treatment Among Arrestees (SANTA) Project.* College Park, MD: Center for Substance Abuse Research (CESAR).

Wooddy, Carroll H. 1934. *The Growth of the Federal Government, 1915–1932.* New York: McGraw-Hill.

Xu, Yili, Mora L. Fiedler, and Karl H. Flaming. 2005. "Discovering the Impact of Community Policing: the Broken

Windows Thesis, Collective Efficacy, and Citizens' Judgment." *Journal of Research in Crime and Delinquency* 42 (2).

Young, Malcolm. 1991. *An Inside Job: Policing and Police Culture in Britain.* Oxford: Clarendon Press.

Zahn, M. A., and M. Bencivengo. 1974. "Violent Death: A Comparison Between Drug Users and Nondrug Users." *Addictive Diseases* 1:283–96.

Zimring, Franklin E. 2007. *The Great American Crime Decline.* New York: Oxford University Press.

Zimring, Franklin E., and Gordon Hawkins. 1997. *Crime is Not the Problem.* New York: Oxford University Press.

Index

drug corner, 66–77, 89–92,
102–6, 130–35, 158–59
drug culture, 48
drug dealers, 48, 71, 76, 115
drug dealing, 66–77. *See also*
drug trade
drug enforcement, cost of,
213n8. *See also* war on drugs
drug-free zone, 114
drug legalization, 86, 187, 189,
191–93, 204n29
drug offenders, as percentage of
prison population, 213n9
drug overdoses, 68–69, 85–86,
189
drug policy: Netherlands,
191–93, 213n12, 214n13; U.S.,
185–93
drug prohibition, 159, 172–77, 187
drugs: cut, 77; "name brands," 68
drug searches, 106
drug tourism, in Netherlands,
192
drug trade, 3, 6, 46–49, 66–77,
89–92, 102–6, 130–35,
158–59, 204n16. *See also* war
on drugs
drunkenness, public, 168

East Baltimore, 3
Eastern District, Baltimore,
10–12; arrest rates, 121,
156–57; drug-free zones, 114;
drug use, 49; homicide rate,
73–75, 203n14; 911 calls,
97–100; and war on drugs,
182–83
Edwards, Edward (governor of
New Jersey), 163
Einstein, Izzy, 166

ethical issues: around drugs,
77–80; in report writing,
50–55
ethnographic research, 6–10
exoticism, 16
"eye fucking," 104

failure to prosecute, 129–36
Federal Bureau of Investigation
(FBI), 71
Federal Bureau of Narcotics,
165, 176
Federal Narcotics Control
Board, 164
field interview, 103
field training, 37–38
field training officers, 38
firearms: in drug trade, 74–75;
requirement to carry, 15, 20.
See also culture of violence
foot patrol, 92–93, 108
force, use of, legal rules for, 23
found property, 72
fraternal organization of police, 35
Frazier, Thomas, 5
frisking, for weapons, 28, 30–31
funerals, of slain officers, 17–18

gangs, 75–76, 204n22
ghetto, 3, 16–17, 38–41. *See also*
Eastern District; high-crime
districts
ghetto culture, 39–41
ghetto language, 60–63
Goffman, Ervin, 41
gonzo journalism, 6–10
Great Depression, 171
gun control, 149
gunman, 66, 70
guns. *See* firearms